PREGNANT TOO SOON

Also by Jeanne Warren Lindsay:

They'll Read If It Matters:
Study Guides for Books About Pregnancy and Parenting

You'll Read If It Matters:
A Student Manual

Parenting Preschoolers:
Curriculum Help and Study Guides
(Teacher's Guide)

Parenting Preschoolers:
Study Guides for Child Care Books
(Student Manual)

PREGNANT TOO SOON

ADOPTION IS AN OPTION

By Jeanne Warren Lindsay

Illustrated by Pam Patterson Morford

About the Author

Jeanne Warren Lindsay is the teacher/coordinator for the ABC Unified School District Teen Mother Program at Tracy High School, Cerritos, California. Most pregnant students in the district choose to attend this class rather than continue at their regular school during pregnancy.

Ms. Lindsay has an M.A. in Anthropology and an M.A. in Home Economics from California State University, Long Beach. Her teaching credentials include General Secondary Life, Pupil Personnel Services, and Administrative. She is a member of the California Alliance Concerned with School Age Parents, and she edits the *CACSAP Newsletter*.

Previous books by Ms. Lindsay include *They'll Read If It Matters: Study Guides for Books About Pregnancy and Parenting; You'll Read If It Matters: A Student Manual; Parenting Preschoolers: Curriculum Help and Study Guides* (for teachers); and *Parenting Preschoolers: Study Guides for Child Care Books* (for students).

Ms. Lindsay and her husband, Bob, have five children.

ISBN 0-88436-778-9
(previously ISBN 0-930934-04-0)
© 1980 by Jeanne Warren Lindsay
All rights reserved. Published 1980

Published by EMC Publishing
180 East Sixth Street
Saint Paul, Minnesota 55101

Printed in the United States of America
0 9 8 7 6 5 4 3 2 1

To All the Courageous Young Women
Who Share Their Lives
On These Pages

T O   M O M

By Jen Myers

Woman who cared, I thank you.
Woman who cared, I dream of you.
I feel us alike, you and I --
More alike than I ever dreamed.
I reach to tell you that I am
*   and that you would be proud.*
I reach to show you my life
*   but not to grab yours.*
I think I know the pain you felt;
I think I feel the love you gave.
You made the right choice.
Woman who cares, I thank you.

(Ms. Myers, who was adopted by her parents
when she was five months old, teaches in a
pregnant minor program in California.)

CONTENTS

FOREWORD

This fine book deals with an extremely sensitive topic -- the decision of whether to rear a child at a very young age or to relinquish the child for adoption. The focus is on the readiness of the young person to parent.

The author assists the reader in realistically evaluating one's capabilities in meeting the physical and emotional needs of the child. This is not an easy task, as one may not fully realize what it means to be a parent until actually faced with the responsibilities of parenthood.

Over the past decade an increasing number of young women have elected to parent at a very young age. Indeed, 90 percent of the pregnant adolescents in the United States keep their babies.

Some teenage parents do an excellent job of child-rearing. However, the majority report that they experience far greater demands than they had anticipated. The adolescents' own maturational processes may make parenting particularly difficult. Because of their youth, these young people often face serious financial, educational, social, and emotional challenges.

Pregnant teens often feel that the decision to release a child is a selfish or uncaring act. Ms. Lindsay presents the decision to relinquish in a far more positive and realistic light, showing that it can be a very loving and mature

decision. Her approach is sensitive to the needs of both
mother and child. This quality of sensitivity and insight is
the result of her experience in working intimately with
childbearing adolescents. Her own nurturant and caring
attitude is evident throughout the book.

The author's professional skill is apparent in the
thoroughness of her exploration of the topic. The ramifica-
tions of adoption, as well as the humanness of the people
involved, are well presented through the use of case studies and interviews.

Those of us who work with pregnant teenagers can
be grateful to Ms. Lindsay for filling a long-time gap. This
book is the first to comprehensively present adoption as a
viable option. It brings balance back into the exploration
of alternatives.

February, 1980   Catherine Monserrat, M.A.
                                Linda Barr, R.N., M.N.
                                Family Life Specialists
                                New Futures School
                                Albuquerque, New Mexico

                                Co-authors:
                                *Teenage Pregnancy, A New
                                    Beginning;*
                                *Working with Childbearing
                                    Adolescents*

FOREWORD

Parenthood can be a choice, a decision based on the desires, needs, and resources of the parents. It is not an easy decision. It is the most intimate, soul searching, growing experience I have ever witnessed.

When I began working with pregnant minors as a program coordinator and counselor, I found few young people exploring the option to adopt.

The first person to share her feelings about adoption with me became my teacher. As I followed her in her own searching of her feelings, support systems, future goals for herself and her child, I, too, had to explore my feelings.

I ran into some old myths, lack of knowledge, and the most intense feelings I have ever experienced. I had to face the old myths, search out information, and allow my feelings to emerge in order to assist this courageous young woman. We both grew.

Students in the program listened, felt, and explored their own feelings as she shared her story. The option to adopt became a more viable option to others.

Reading this book offers you, whether you are a pregnant woman, a staff member of a support service, a father-to-be or a grandparent-to-be, or perhaps an adoptive parent, the opportunity to face your myths, collect accurate information concerning the process, and explore your feelings. The emotions you will experience in the process may be intense: joy, fear, sadness, pride. Allow your feelings to emerge, talk about them, and watch yourself grow.

The life stories of these young people have touched me personally. I have tremendous admiration and gratitude to them for allowing me to share their experiences.

February, 1980   Jean Colwell, Counselor
                                San Juan Unified School District
                                Sacramento, California

PREFACE

At least one million teenagers in the United States get pregnant each year according to Planned Parenthood statistics. About 600,000 of these young women give birth. Thirty thousand girls younger than 15 become pregnant annually, and nearly half of them deliver their babies.

Most (94 percent) of these young mothers keep their babies at home to rear themselves. About 2.5 percent send the baby to live with relatives or friends. Only 3.5 percent relinquish their babies for adoption. These figures include married as well as single mothers. Of the unmarried pregnant teenagers, five percent place the baby with relatives or friends, and about eight percent relinquish their infants for adoption.

All of these statistics are taken from *11 Million Teenagers: What Can Be Done About the Epidemic of Adolescent Pregnancies in the United States.* The booklet was published in 1976 by the Alan Guttmacher Institute, Research and Development Division of Planned Parenthood Federation of America.

I have worked with pregnant teenagers during seven years of teaching a self-contained day-long public school class which is offered as an option for pregnant students. After spending many full school days with each of these young women during her pregnancy, a close bond is often created between us.

Because we have an Infant Center on campus which
cares for their babies while they attend school, many young
mothers choose to stay at our small alternative school after
they leave the "pregnant" class. (Each student may stay in
the special class until the end of the semester in which her
baby is born.) Most of these high school mothers continue
coming to my room for a daily parenting class while they are
attending the high school.

I see many of these young women doing a good job of
parenting. I know of no research "proving" that a 16-year-
old is necessarily a less able mother than is a woman of 25.
The young women I know care a great deal about their babies,
give them lots of love, and often cope remarkably well with
the responsibilities and extra problems associated with being a very young and, often, a single mother.

After this close association with some 250 pregnant
teenagers, however, I am disturbed that the majority do not
appear to *choose* motherhood. They simply assume that because they are pregnant and have chosen not to have an abortion, they *must* become mothers.

I can empathize with them -- I have five children,
and they weren't all "planned" babies. My husband and I
never considered relinquishing any of our children for adoption, and I don't think it makes a lot of difference in feelings
that I was 22 and married when I had my first baby. Being
15 and single doesn't eliminate those feelings of love and
caring that most people have for their babies.

Many of the million teenagers who become pregnant
each year make a choice. Slightly more than one out of four
terminates pregnancy through induced abortion. This is a
choice which, I think, must be available to every woman who
is pregnant. Every woman should know she has this choice.

However, abortion is seldom mentioned in this book.
By the time I meet them, the young women with whom I work
have already decided against abortion. Otherwise they
would not be enrolling in a class for pregnant students.
Their remaining and ever-narrowing choices are marriage
(sometimes), single motherhood, and adoption. If I had
written *Pregnant Too Soon* twenty years ago when most

pregnant teenagers were relinquishing their babies for adoption, this would have been a very different book. I probably would have discussed ways of dealing with, perhaps encouraging, single motherhood, because at that time it wasn't the accepted thing to do.

Today *adoption* is not "the thing to do" according to many people, both adults and teenagers. I'm uncomfortable with both approaches -- either expecting *all* teenagers to relinquish or expecting *each one* to keep her baby. I think the leading lady in this drama, the young mother, too often has been -- and still is -- pressured into making a decision because *other people* think it's right for her.

But *she* must make this decision herself! Since our culture today appears to accept single motherhood more easily than it accepts adoption, much of our literature is devoted to single parenting. This book is an attempt to even the score a little -- an attempt to show adoption as a viable option to ill-timed parenthood.

"When I was thinking about adoption, I wished there had been more to read," a student recently commented. "You gave me a few things, but I wanted to know more about how other people *felt*. I read a lot of books about how the adoption agencies work, what happens afterward, etc., but there was nothing that compared the feelings of people who gave their babies up for adoption and people who kept their babies. I wanted to compare those feelings."

In this book, young women who relinquished their babies for adoption and young women who kept their children share some of their feelings about and attitudes toward adoption. All the stories about and quotes from teenagers are real. All the events described actually happened. Names and minor details have been changed to protect the privacy of the young people involved. Only exception to these masked identities is Julie Gomoll whose story appears in Chapter One.

Pregnant Too Soon is certainly not a plea for all pregnant teenagers -- or all those under 18 -- or even all those under 15 -- to release their babies for adoption. It is, rather, a book dedicated to the principle that parenthood is such a great experience for many people that it deserves to be a *chosen* state of being!

Many pregnant teenagers do not realize that adoption is, indeed, an option.

———————————

A great many people have helped make this book possible. Most important, of course, are the young women who share their lives in these pages. They wanted to help. Over and over I heard, "Perhaps my story will help someone else."

Jean Colwell, for five years coordinator of the Young Parents Program in the San Juan Unified School District, Sacramento, California, shared her techniques for helping young women make responsible decisions. More important, she shared her feelings of love and admiration for the courageous teenagers with whom she has worked. In a very real sense, this book is partly hers.

Charlotte De Armond, State Director of Public Affairs for Children's Home Society of California, shared a great deal of information about adoption. She also checked the completed manuscript, as did Janice Wills, social worker for the Los Angeles County Department of Adoptions.

Many others discussed adoption with me. I especially appreciate the help I received from David Leavitt, Patricia Swiebert, Sen Speroff, Cathy Warner, Maria Vargas-Pyle, Hector Fregoso, Catherine Monserrat, Linda Barr, Merle Church, and Nancy Walsworth. Perhaps even more helpful were the comments from adult adoptees and adoptive parents.

Don Teague and Larry Church provided valuable help in editing the manuscript.

But it is the young women themselves who really wrote this book. They are beautiful and courageous people, and I care a great deal about them.

Two other beautiful people are Bob and Erin who helped by being tolerant and supportive during this year of writing *Pregnant Too Soon*. I love them.

February, 1980   Jeanne Lindsay, M.A.

CHAPTER 1

To Be or Not to Be— A School Age Parent

Many women, including a lot of teenagers, have unplanned pregnancies.

More than one million teenagers in the United States become pregnant each year. About two-thirds of these pregnancies are unplanned, according to Planned Parenthood's booklet, *11 Million Teenagers: What Can Be Done About the Epidemic of Adolescent Pregnancies in the United States* (1976).

Only ten percent of the pregnancies among unmarried teenagers are intended, perhaps less. The ten percent figure is from a survey of unmarried mothers *after* they had their babies. Whether they wanted to become pregnant before they conceived is unknown.

Babies and sex perhaps should *not* be related. An 18-year dose of parenthood is a rather odd follow-up to ten or fifteen minutes of sex. But, since the two -- sex and babies -- are very closely related, it is not surprising that so many of us experience unplanned, sometimes unwanted pregnancies.

Twenty years ago many pregnant teenagers relinquished (gave up, released, surrendered) their babies for adoption. An unmarried adolescent who became pregnant was often hustled off to Aunt Agathà's home in Missouri where she lived until her baby was born.

Usually the young mother didn't see her baby at all. It was placed for adoption with a family she would never meet. The entire event was wrapped in secrecy. Her friends were told she was simply vacationing with Aunt Agatha. She was urged to forget the whole episode and get back to her "normal" life as a teenager.

Within the past ten years, this picture has changed. Women of all ages have a legal right to an abortion during the early months of pregnancy. Each year about one-fourth of those million teenage pregnancies end in induced abortion. Each year almost half of the 30,000 girls under 15 who become pregnant get abortions.

But more than 600,000 teenagers give birth each year. (About 14 percent of the million pregnancies end in spontaneous miscarriage.) Very few of these young women relinquish their babies for adoption. About five percent of the babies born to unmarried teenagers are sent to live with relatives or friends. Less than eight percent (16,380 each year) go through the legal process of releasing their infants for adoption. (All of these statistics are taken from *11 Million Teenagers.*)

Technically, the word "relinquishment" refers to the birth parents legally signing over (giving up) their child to an adoption agency. The agency then places the child with its adoptive family. Until the child is placed, the agency has custody of the child, not the birth parents.

"Consent to adopt" is the term used to refer to birth parents legally releasing their child directly to its adoptive parents as is done in independent adoption. (See Chapter Four.)

Throughout this book, the terms "relinquish," "release," "consent to adopt," "give up," and "surrender" are used interchangeably. Each refers to the legal act of releasing one's birth child for adoption by another family.

Sometimes in the past the term "natural parent" has been used to refer to the parent who gave birth to a baby, then released that baby for adoption. Some people feel this implies the adoptive parents must be "unnatural"! To avoid this connotation, *birth* parent is the preferred term.

PARENTHOOD BY CHOICE?

If almost 200,000 unmarried teenagers 17 years old or younger, and another 100,000 who married after pregnancy occurred *choose* to keep their babies to rear themselves, their decision must be respected. It is certainly possible for a young single mother to do a fine job of parenting, especially if she has a good support system within her family.

But is that choice consciously made? Or is becoming a mother often simply acceptance of what is, or seems to be -- that if one is pregnant and doesn't get an abortion, one will usually have a baby (true), and therefore raise that baby oneself (not necessarily true)?

Many young women are "successful" mothers. They give their children the care they need, sometimes at great sacrifice to themselves. They love their children deeply. But it is difficult to know who will be a good parent and who will not, whether that parent is single or married, 15 or 25 years old. Some 25 year old parents neglect their children. Sometimes a 15-year-old does a beautiful job of mothering.

Nevertheless, school age parents often have a far more difficult time parenting a child (or children) than do older parents. Julie Gomoll, a young mother living in Portland, Oregon, wrote "And Baby Makes Two" for *Paper Rose,* a CETA publication in Portland (October 31, 1978). Following are excerpts from her article:

I remember being pregnant at 15. The only thing on my mind was that I wanted to keep my "baby."

Sure, babies are easy to care for, needing only feeding, changing and hugs, but now I have a 3 year old son, a roommate, and someone who needs respect. Unlike a baby, he needs to share most of the decisions concerning him. When I have to be at a meeting or go to a class, my son must be interested in going to daycare too.

Performing the tasks of a parent is not always rewarding and enjoyable. People get into parenting with little information on what it takes. I wanted to be a mom so that I could be on my own.

Somehow, becoming a teenager flipped a switch for me. That little taste of freedom: being able to stay out until 10 p.m., to go to parties and on dates was exciting. But I wanted more. I did not want to answer to anyone -- not my folks, not my yelling and screaming brothers and sisters, and not my teachers. When my pregnancy test came back positive, it was my magical chance to be my own family. I could be my own boss.

Well, I've been my own boss for over two years now and it's scary. When I'm late for work, I can't blame it on my Mom for not waking me. When my term paper isn't finished, I can't make my folks babysit all night -- so I can't do it. I hate responsibility. Freedom has turned out to be something different than what I bargained for. What I did bargain for were all the goodies and none of the work.

I don't recommend motherhood as the way to independence.

POSSIBLE RESULTS OF EARLY PREGNANCY

Extra problems for teenagers often start during pregnancy. Adolescents are much more apt to have toxemia and/or anemia during pregnancy than are older women. Both are serious health problems. Teenage mothers' babies are much more likely to be premature and to have low birth weight. Other health problems may occur, often the result of poor nutrition, lack of prenatal care, or simply because of the physical immaturity of the young woman.

Eight out of ten teenage mothers never finish high school. Most have not had a chance to obtain job skills or work experience. A California study of single parent families was carried out by the Rand Corporation (1977: *AFDC Caseload and the Job Market in California: Selected Issues* by Abrahamse, De Ferranti, and Fleischauer). The study compared single parents under 25 who had not completed high school with those who had.

Ninety percent of the single parents in the study who had dropped out of school were on welfare. But the number on welfare was cut in half if the single parent had completed high school!

A study quoted by Planned Parenthood in *11 Million Teenagers* showed twice as many women who gave birth at age 16 or 17 were poor as were mothers who waited until they were at least 20 to have their first child. Fully one-third of the mothers who had their first baby before they were 15 were below the federal poverty line.

Julie continues:

I feel sad, angry, frustrated, and selfish when I think I brought a child of mine into the world when I was financially unstable, had no career goals, and no job experience. And because of these reasons, I was not emotionally ready to be a mom.

In three years I had to learn to cook, do laundry and keep house, including learning how to keep budgets, balance a checking account, pay the utility bills, find good babysitters and afford them, not to mention finding beds, cribs, chairs, tables, pots, skillets, forks, knives, spoons, baby clothes, blocks, chalk boards, and everything else.

I had to learn to drive, shop for food, find a job, decide on a career, and then find out how I could manage establishing that career.

I had to and am still learning how to handle the system -- welfare and its workers, employers, taxes and HUD, etc. Going to school, being a mom, and working is so much harder than I anticipated way back when, and I live it every day.

MARRIAGE OFTEN NO SOLUTION

Teenage marriage does not often last long enough to solve these problems. Brides who marry before they are 18 are three times as apt to have their marriages break up later as are women who marry in their early 20s. In fact, three out of every five pregnant teen brides are divorced within six years.

"Out-of-Wedlock Births Up 75 Percent Among Younger Teens" headlines an item in Planned Parenthood's *11 Million Teenagers*. But "out-of-wedlock" may well be a healthy trend (compared to too-early marriage) -- healthy from the standpoint of people coping with pregnancy and parenthood.

A married student is much more likely to drop out of school after the birth of her baby. Sometimes she does so at the insistance of her husband! Recently a 16-year-old called to say she wouldn't be returning to school after the birth of her baby. "My husband says I have enough education to be a housewife," she said.

The young woman who is married probably won't go to work if her husband is working. She may have another baby within a year. (Single mothers in our class almost never have a repeat pregnancy until they are married and want another baby.)

Yet five years later this married student has a high

risk (60 percent!) of being single again. If she is, she may
have no high school diploma, no job skills, and must support
and care for not just one, but two or even three small children.

When Brenda called about enrolling in the special
class for pregnant students, she said she and her boy friend
were going to be married. She had dropped out of school a
couple of months earlier when she discovered she was pregnant. She had just heard of the class, and thought perhaps
she could earn her diploma before delivery.

But her pregnancy was hard on her. She missed quite
a bit of school that winter, then moved in with Manuel soon
after their baby was born. Brenda explained:

ALL I could think about was how great it would
be to get married. I thought we were madly in
Love and that marriage would solve everything.
Manuel got a job and we set our wedding date.
When Stacey was three months old, we got married.

I didn't know it yet, but I was pregnant
again on my wedding day. And that was the pregnancy I didn't want to tell anyone about! I felt
rotten again and Stacey took a Lot of time. The
apartment was always a mess, and we didn't have
enough money.

Manuel Lost his job the week after the doctor
told me I was pregnant. We got unemployment for
a while, but he didn't find work. I don't think
he tried very hard. He started Lying around the
apartment all day -- I thought I would go crazy!

The unemployment ran out so we had to go back
on welfare. And I had thought marriage would
mean no more welfare. . .We were kicked out of one
apartment because we couldn't pay the rent -- and
that was because welfare made a mistake and we
didn't get our check on time.

But we couldn't get our apartment back. We
found another one, in a worse part of town.

Meghan was born two days after Christmas. I

went home to my mother's for a couple of weeks.
I couldn't have made it otherwise. Then I went
back to our apartment with the two kids. Manuel
got a job, but it lasted only a month. We were
back on welfare.

This dragged on for almost a year. I would
tell Manuel to leave. Sometimes he would go,
but he'd be back within a day or two. Finally I
told him I was through. By then my nerves were
shot. I went back to my mother's, and she said
she would keep the kids for a while until I got
myself together.

It was at this point that Brenda turned up at school
again. She had decided she had to have her high school diploma and some job skills. She was already 19, so she
wasn't admitted back into the high school. She started
working on her remaining academic requirements in the
Adult School Learning Lab. She spent the rest of her time
in the Office Occupations Center learning secretarial skills.

One day she volunteered to talk to the Teen Mother
Program students. She told her story, and stressed that
marriage doesn't solve everything. "I thought I was so
lucky because I could get married," she said wryly, "and
now look at me -- two kids and not even a high school diploma."

But Brenda's story has a happy ending -- rather,
beginning. She called a few months later to announce elat-
edly, "I have a job' I start Monday morning, and it pays
pretty well. I think the kids and I can move into our own
apartment in a month or so."

The following semester she took time off from work
to speak to the new group of girls in class. She discussed
the dangers in getting married because of pregnancy, then
went on to speak enthusiastically about the need for a diploma and job skills, and of the satisfaction she's getting from
working to support her two little girls. "It's hard work,
and we still don't have much money," she concluded. "But
we're a family again, the three of us, and I much prefer it
this way."

"Will you get married again?" a student asked.

"Probably, if the right man comes along," she answered. "But I'll never marry again because I think I 'have' to."

––––––––––

The high school mother who remains single, if she continues her education and obtains job skills, is apt to be in a much better position three or four years later than is her formerly-married classmate. No wonder so many teenagers decide pregnancy is not enough reason to get married!

WHO IS MY MOTHER?

If a young single mother has the support of her family, she is usually better off then is the young woman completely on her own. However, this, too, can become a difficult situation.

Anita, who released her son for adoption two years ago, spoke of her concern for her friend, Claudia, and for Claudia's daughter, Nichole:

Claudia and I are almost the same age. She came into the Teen Mother Program a few weeks after I did, and we've been good friends ever since. The way I see her today and the way I see me is

that I made the best choice. I only hope she
feels she did the right thing for her.

Her baby is never with her -- she's never
home. Nichole hardly knows who her mother is because her grandmother takes care of her. About
the only time they're together is at night when
the baby sleeps in Claudia's room. Claudia is
one of my best friends, yet she never brings Nichole with her when she comes over. And Nichole
isn't a little brat, she's a neat little girl.

Claudia says, "Nichole hardly ever listens to
me. She listens to my mother." Yet she's here
until 10 or 11 p.m. While I like to see her, I
would think she would want to be with her daughter. But then she's young.

When she thought about moving in with her
sister, she said she wanted to move in *without*
Nichole. She said, "I go to school and I go to
work, then I go home. I'm too tired to face taking care of Nichole. My folks scream at me and
it's so bad sometimes I just leave."

I told her that when she does leave with
Nichole, it will break her parents' hearts, and
she agreed. Her Dad absolutely idolizes NIchole.

I think we're alike in a lot of ways. I hope
I would have taken more of the responsibility if
I had kept Elizabeth. Claudia really isn't. . .
she's giving the responsibility to her Mother and
Dad. There's no way I would expect my parents to
take care of my child.

Having, caring for, and loving children are joyful
situations for many people. It is an especially joyful happening if the timing is "right." Parenthood at 17 -- or even 15
-- may be right for some people. But postponing parenthood
for a few years could make it more joyful for some of those
many teenagers who each year keep their babies to raise
themselves.

Adoption is an option!

CHAPTER 2

Are YOU Ready for Parenthood

How would you feel if you were a pregnant teenager? Or if your girl friend were pregnant?

Or. . .if you are pregnant now, how do you really feel about parenting a child? Do you think you have a choice *now* between being or not being a mother?

Assuming you have decided not to have an abortion, do you think any discussion of whether or not to parent a child concerns you? Do you still have options?

Perhaps your friends and/or your parents simply assume that because you are pregnant, you're going to have a baby to raise. Suzanne, a pregnant 16–year–old, wrote:

I wanted to get an abortion but I didn't have the money. Now that I'm this far along, I just have to take what Mother Nature gave me and treat it right.

Before I got pregnant, I planned to be an actress and marry a doctor. But now Kent can't go to medical school, and I'm not even sure I'll be able to go to college to study drama.

If I had one wish, I'd wish I could start my life over beginning at age 15. I would rather have a baby when my career allows it.

Suzanne doesn't believe she has a choice. For her,

motherhood *must* follow pregnancy.

Some teenagers' feelings about abortion versus adoption are interesting. One girl said, "No, I would never give my baby up for adoption. In my opinion, if others want to do that, they should have an abortion instead of giving the baby away to a stranger.

I have talked with several girls who were agonizing over the abortion decision. Jeanette told me she really didn't want to have a baby because she had seen two of her sisters "ruin their lives" (her words) by having babies when they were 15 or 16. She didn't want to be like them. But she also explained that she considered abortion wrong, that she thought of it as murder.

When adoption was mentioned as another option, she quickly said, "Oh, no. If I go through the nine months of pregnancy, I certainly won't give the baby away." Jeanette finally decided to have an abortion.

I respect her right to that abortion. But I do question her value system that says abortion is better than letting another family rear that baby. So many couples desperately want a baby but can't give birth to their own -- couples who probably would be able to give an adopted child a tremendous amount of love and care.

Many pregnant teenagers choose *not* to get an abortion. About three out of four adolescents continue their pregnancies. So how do girls (and their boy friends) make the heavy decision of whether to raise their baby themselves or place it for adoption? Is it usually an emotional decision -- "I would *never* give my baby up for adoption"?

Or, as Diana put it, "I knew right away I would keep it. . .it's part of me. At first I thought I could give it up for adoption, but then I thought I couldn't stand knowing I have a baby out there somewhere."

These are emotional decisions, but they show the extreme importance of the mothers' feelings. These feelings must be seriously considered, of course.

But good parenting includes more than feelings.

QUESTIONS TO PONDER

Loving your baby is crucial, perhaps the most crucial aspect of parenting. But having enough money to feed him/her, living in a place you consider OK for both of you, being able to provide medical care for you and your baby -- these unexciting things are also important.

There are other questions to consider. Do you think it is necessary for a child to have a father as well as a mother?

What about *you*? Can you continue your education if you are responsible for a child? Can you prepare for the kind of job you want?

Are you willing to give up a great deal of time to care for your child? Are you planning how you can take most of this responsibility, or are you expecting someone else to do much of the work?

Close your eyes and think of yourself as the mother (or father) of a two-year-old who is extremely lively and says "No" a great deal. How do you feel about parenting a toddler who often does his own thing? Toddlers are quite different from the infant who, while she needs lots of cuddling and physical care, sleeps a lot and doesn't defy you.

Still with your eyes closed, think about your child.
Is she usually a baby? Or do you anticipate the toddler and
preschool stages? Perhaps think about her going to kindergarten? How old will you be then?

Surely most people don't think that having a baby is
punishment. However, it is sometimes suggested that if a
girl gets pregnant, she should pay for her "wrongdoing" by
raising the baby. A student said, "I will never give my baby up for adoption -- I made a mistake and I'm going to live
with my mistake."

Kirsten, however, discusses in Chapter Four why
she has an entirely opposite opinion. She feels that placing a baby with parents who want him very much is one way,
as she puts it, of "turning something bad into something
good."

BETH'S FAMILY

Beth was pregnant several years ago when she was
a high school senior. Recently I visited her. Obviously
she is enjoying her two children, her husband, and her
home. When Eddie was born, Beth and Scott were ready
for parenthood.

Eddie, 3, and Shannon, $1\frac{1}{2}$, were asleep when I arrived. About 15 minutes later Shannon toddled out. She
smiled broadly as she gestured toward the cookie jar. Her
mother changed her diaper, then handed her a cookie.

A few minutes later Eddie wandered out looking
like a thunder cloud. "He wakes up slowly just like me,"
his mother commented. After a brief rest on his mother's
lap, he, too, was ready for a cookie. Then the two blonde,
blue-eyed children went out to play in the hot California
sunshine.

Beth chatted about her children ("They're into everything now!") and about Scott. They celebrated their
fourth wedding anniversary last month, and she reported
proudly that he was recently promoted to a better job.
"We think we can afford a new car soon," she added with
a smile.

We heard a commotion in the kitchen. Beth went in to check. I heard her say in a startled tone, "Is Shannon in *there*?" She laughed and called me. She and Eddie were standing by a little cupboard but Shannon wasn't in sight. Eddie giggled as he opened the door of their toy cupboard. There was tiny Shannon, curled up on the second shelf. . . she had crammed herself into a space about eight inches high and perhaps two feet wide! She, too, giggled as she climbed out of her hiding place.

Obviously Beth, who was 22 in April, and Scott have a highly satisfying life with their children.

Five years ago Beth gave birth to another child, a little boy. She talked about that pregnancy and her difficult decision to place him for adoption:

It was the week after my 16th birthday that I first thought I was pregnant. I tried to ignore the whole idea, but as time went on, I knew I was indeed pregnant. I was scared to death to say anything to anybody.

I was at least four months pregnant before I even told Sam. We were still dating, but by then I knew things weren't going to work out between us. He told me I should get an abortion -- he even offered to pay for it -- but it was too late for the suction method, and besides, I just didn't feel right about that.

So I wore baggy clothes and hoped no one would notice. A couple of months later -- I must have been at least six months pregnant -- my Mom got a good side view of me as I was going out one evening. The next morning she said, "You're pregnant, aren't you?"

I said, "No." I just couldn't tell her or my father because I knew it would kill them.

"Well, I know you are," she replied.

So she cried and I cried. . .Then she made an appointment for me to see our doctor.

I told her I didn't want to continue school where I was, but neither did I want to go to the special school in our district. It had a pretty bad reputation. After a lot of discussion with her and my Dad, we decided to talk with our close friends, Alice and Bob, who had recently moved from our neighborhood to a new home about 80 miles away. I used to babysit a lot for them.

Alice and Bob told us they had heard about a good school program for pregnant students in their district. They suggested I enroll in this school and live with them until I delivered. So I moved in with them the next week. My Mom told my friends I was visiting my cousin in Arizona. Surprisingly, we pulled it off. Most of my friends never knew I was pregnant.

When did you decide to give the baby up for adoption?

My folks kind of influenced me at first. They didn't tell me what to do, but my Mom said, "You're going to release it for adoption, aren't you?"

So I said, "Well, yes, whatever you want." I had found out I was still alive after telling them I was pregnant, and I wasn't going to push my luck right then! But as I thought about it, it sounded like a good idea. I wanted to finish high school, perhaps go on to college. I just didn't think it would work with a baby.

It was purely my decision. I knew that. I knew that in our family I really couldn't raise the baby and do what I wanted to do. I did ask my Mom how she would feel if I kept it. She told me she would love the baby, but she would not raise it. She said if I needed a babysitter, I would have to find someone else. I knew she meant it. By then, I really knew inside that I was going to relinquish for adoption, but I wanted to find out how they might feel if I did decide to keep it.

My Dad had told me I didn't have to move in with Alice and Bob. He told me that if my friends were nasty to me, they weren't good friends anyhow. But I wanted to go there. I still think it was the right thing to do.

I lived with Alice and Bob and attended the special school for about three months. I felt pretty good most of the time so I helped Alice take care of their two little boys. I also learned to cook -- something I hadn't done at home much.

One cold night early in March I went into labor. My little boy was born late the next afternoon. The doctor didn't think I should see my baby. But I insisted, and of course they let me. He was beautiful.

Have you ever regretted your decision?

No, I haven't. I suppose I could if I thought a lot about it. Of course I think about him, but I have my family now and he has his. He'll start kindergarten this fall. I do wish I knew what he looks like, if he has many friends, how his parents treat him.

Adoption is a big deal. But I think maybe it isn't as big a deal as some girls think it is. Of course it's hard giving up a baby you have carried for nine months. But life goes on. I think about him every now and then, but I don't let it get to me.

ROBIN'S STORY

That same day I visited with another young mother. Robin is 19 and her son, Stu, is $3\frac{1}{2}$. Robin, who became pregnant at 15, talked to an adoption counselor. She decided, however, to keep her baby. She, too, knows she made the right decision -- for her.

Robin is living in a city about 40 miles from my home. When I telephoned her, she suggested we meet for lunch at her favorite restaurant. She had spoken enthusiastically about her new job selling real estate. She assured me her time was her own and she could see me for as long as we liked.

She was waiting when I walked in -- even more lovely, taller, and slimmer than I remembered. As we ate pizza, she talked about her life during the past two years, a time when I had seen her only occasionally. Stu was born while she was in tenth grade. He stayed in the Infant Center on campus while his mother worked furiously on her high school graduation requirements. And she made it -- a year early!

Soon after that she and her family moved to their present home a couple of miles outside the city. She had attended the community college these past two years. She had also earned her realtor's license.

For a brief time last year Robin and Stu lived with a man, but that didn't work out so they came back home. She reminisced:

> Living away those few months made a differ-
> ence in my relationship with my Mom. I loved
> having my own place, being on my own. We had a
> tight budget, and I learned a lot -- cooking,
> cleaning, managing. I did enjoy it, but I had
> moved in with Abe more for convenience -- to
> get away from home -- than for love. And that
> doesn't work!

> So I came back home. But now my Mom knows
> I can make it on my own, that I'm not a child.
> That's the big difference in our relationship.

"What's it really like, being the single mother of a $3\frac{1}{2}$ year old son?"

> Stu has been a joy. He talks at least a
> mile a minute. . .Would you believe he and I sit
> around and just chat? We can have a conversa-
> tion for 45 minutes! How many mothers can do
> that with a 3½-year-old? He's very smart, a
> little mature for his age, I think. He has

never known what it's like having a father and he
has adjusted well.

It's neat having him around. I don't feel he
has been a hindrance in my life, perhaps because
I haven't known anything else for so long. Maybe
he does put a damper on my social life, but then
I hang around mostly with people who enjoy Stu,
and he usually goes along with me. We go camping
and do lots of things together. My mother takes
care of him while I work, but she seldom does any
other babysitting.

"How did you feel about being pregnant?"

Fat! I knew I was pregnant two weeks after I
conceived. I told the baby's father about a week
later.

"Well, you can do one of two things," he said.

"Oh?" I replied.

"Yes, you can either get an abortion or you

can marry me."

"Marry you? Sorry," I said. He vanished soon after that. I think he is in the service now, but I will never press charges. I don't need him. Physically he is Stu's father, but mentally, no."

"How did your parents react?"

I didn't tell them until I couldn't fit into my clothes any longer -- by then I was about five months pregnant. My mother cried, thought it was her fault. I kept saying, "How can it be your fault? I'm the one who screwed around!"

Since my aunt works in an adoption agency, naturally my mother made an appointment for me to talk to a counselor there. I talked with the worker (not my aunt) for nearly two hours. She told me that a lot of unwed mothers my age keep their babies at first, then relinquish them later because they can't cope -- like two years down the road they give them up.

I took it all in. I listened and then I said, "OK, but I have made my decision."

When I told her I was going to keep the baby, she said I should go home and think about it. But I had already decided. I kept him -- probably because I'm headstrong and because I'm me! And I don't regret my decision.

When I brought him home from the hospital, of course it was hard work taking care of him. But I was expecting that. I'm the oldest in a family of five children. I was my littlest brother's mother, practically. It wasn't anything new to me to change a diaper, to hold, to cuddle. Perhaps that's why I didn't worry and think, "Oh, my God, how will I do this?" I had already had a lot of responsibility -- my mother would have gone nuts if I hadn't helped her with my little brothers.

What always fascinated and awed me was that this baby was an extension of myself. I could help form him into the kind of person I wanted him to be, caring, happy, able to go through anything and come out all right. Thinking about all that responsibility didn't scare me. It awed me. It is a whole new thing -- having a new baby means he is totally dependent on you for his *life*!

Parenting Stu didn't work well because of good luck. It worked well because I made it -- I worked -- and am working -- hard at being a good parent.

Enthusiastic as Robin is about motherhood, she is absolutely sure she doesn't want another child. In fact, she is so sure that she recently had a tubal ligation (operation which should make it impossible for her to become pregnant again).

ERIN'S LIFE

Not all young mothers feel so positive about early motherhood as Robin does.

Erin's lovely Joanna is almost two years old. She has been coming to "school" at the Infant Center since she was two weeks old. Erin will graduate soon. She then plans to continue her education and become a teacher.

Erin, who obviously loves Joanna dearly, and who does an excellent job of mothering her little daughter, discussed her experiences recently:

I wish I had been married and had waited longer to get pregnant. It's awfully hard raising her by myself.

It's harder as she gets older. When she was born, she was fussed over by my mother and my grandmother. They helped a lot at first. So did my friends. Everybody wanted to babysit for me

at first, but by the time she was seven or eight
months old, they lost interest in her. Most of
my friends quit coming to my house after that. I
guess Joanna just got too old for them.

When I was pregnant, I thought my mother
would help more than she does. It's been worse
than I expected. I take care of my little sister
a lot on weekends, but my Mom almost never baby-
sits Joanna. I either have to take her with me
wherever I go or stay home. During the past week
she hasn't been napping at all during the day --
she's awake all day long, she's cutting her mo-
lars, and she's very fussy. As she gets older,
she's harder to handle. She throws temper tan-
trums, and when she gets really frustrated, she
bites.

"What do you see ahead for yourself?"

Hopefully I will get my education and be a
teacher. When Joanna graduates from the Infant
Center when she's two, I can put her in the other Children's Center here in the district while
I go on to school. I would like to get married,
but if I do, I will still go ahead with my education. I couldn't sit home and take care of a
house all day long!

"Do you have any advice for a young, pregnant teenager?"

First I would ask her what she thinks she
wants to do with the rest of her life. Then I
would tell her how hard it is to have a baby
and still try to do what you want. We have
child care here at school, and still it's hard.
It must be really bad if you don't have that.
I would remind her how important it is to go to
school.

Then I would ask, "Do you want the baby or
not?" If she is already five months pregnant, I
would tell her she has only two options: give
the baby up, or keep it and take care of it.

CONSIDER ALL OPTIONS

If you are young and pregnant, think about the good and the not-so-good things about early parenthood. To help your thinking, write down the good and the bad things about each possible choice. Each pregnant girl who has decided against abortion still has at least two choices -- keeping the baby vs. placing him for adoption. Some girls can also choose between staying single and getting married.

Mark either two or three columns on a sheet of paper, depending on how many choices you have. Now write down all the good things about raising a child -- whether you are single or are/might be married. In another column write down the good things about not having a baby to care for at this point in your life.

On a second sheet of paper, jot down the things you don't like about each of your possible choices.

Now, which choice seems to have more positive things going for you?

While you are pregnant you can't make a legally binding decision to release your baby for adoption. According
to law, you must wait until after delivery to sign relinquishment papers. But it's important to consider all your options
long before that time.

The following comments come from teenagers who
had to make decisions concerning early unplanned pregnancy:

Sally, while she was still pregnant, commented:

At first I was really scared, but now I'm
happy about having a baby. My parents wanted
me to get an abortion. . .then they pushed
adoption, but I wouldn't consider either one.

I'm worried whether or not I can provide a
good life for the baby. It makes me unhappy,
though, the way everyone lectures me. They say
I'm stupid for ruining my life. But I decided
to have the baby regardless of what my parents
think or what anyone else thinks.

When everything is going right and I feel
up, I'm happy. I just hope I can still have
freedom after the baby is born.

Sue, an 18-year-old with a two year old child, suggests:

Well, I think if you are really ready to
have a child, that's neat. But you should
think of the things you have to give up (especially if you're single) because with a baby
you can't always do the things you're used to
doing. Sometimes things can get to you after a
while.

A young woman who chose adoption for her child
writes:

If pregnant, please consider *your* future
and your baby's -- consider adoption. I released my little girl two years ago when she
was born -- and I'm glad I did.

Diana, who doesn't feel she has had a chance to consider her options, explains:

When I was pregnant, I thought my relationship with Jim would last. I didn't think about adoption until Tina was about five months old. I wanted to (consider adoption) really bad by then, but I didn't have anybody to talk to about it.

A baby needs parents that are a little older and ready to settle down. . .they could do more things with her and spend more time with her. Now, me, I still want to go out -- there is so much out there that I want to do and see.

I tried to talk to my Mom but she said, "How could you do that?" She is so afraid of what people might think. But I think it would be better for Tina to have two parents.

Shawna, who is the 19 year old mother of two children and is married to the father of her second baby, said:

Having children at a young age is very satisfying to me, but sometimes I wish I had waited. I love my children and I wouldn't give them up for anything.

But I don't advise anyone who has big plans to get pregnant too young because your child should always come first. If you have plans for the future, sometimes you can't spend enough time with your kids.

"AM I PARENT MATERIAL?"

"Am I Parent Material?" is a leaflet distributed by the National Alliance for Optional Parenthood. The questionnaire from this leaflet is reprinted on page 161 of this book. It contains questions to be considered by people deciding whether or not to have a child at this time.

The questions are meant simply to give you ideas to think about. Of course there are no "right" answers and no "grades." As the pamphlet states, "You *do* have a choice.

Check out what you know and give it some thought. Then do what seems right for you."

The questionnaire can help an unmarried pregnant teenager or a couple expecting a baby to sort out their feelings concerning keeping the child or releasing it for adoption (or having an abortion, if time permits).

The same questionnaire is, of course, also helpful for couples who aren't yet expecting a child. Almost everyone would agree that it is much easier for such a couple to decide not to have children now than it is for the woman who is already pregnant.

But even if you are pregnant now, you, too, have that choice. . .

CHAPTER 3

How Adoption Works—
Agencies

Many young girls who are unintentionally pregnant talk to adoption agency counselors simply because they want to talk to someone. They may not be planning to place their babies for adoption. But they know a counselor can often help them sort out their feelings and concerns.

If you are worried about an unplanned pregnancy, or you aren't quite sure of your decision regarding your child's future, you can talk things over with a trained counselor. Look in the yellow pages of your telephone book under "Adoption." You will probably find one or more listings if you live in an urban area. You can also contact your state or local child welfare agency for information.

Two kinds of adoption services are available -- agency and independent. Independent adoption, in which the birth parents place their baby directly with adoptive parents, will be discussed in the next chapter.

In agency adoption, birth parents relinquish (surrender, release) their child to the adoption agency. The agency then places the child with a carefully selected family. In most agency adoptions, the birth parents never meet the adoptive parents. Birth parents don't know their baby's new parents' names, nor do the adoptive parents know theirs.

Birth parents who deal with an agency, however,

usually have some choice in the family who will receive their child. They generally will not know the family's identity, but their caseworker will describe one, usually several, would-be adoptive families.

These are families already approved for placement of a child by the agency, families which the agency thinks would be suitable for this particular baby. The birth mother -- and father, if he is involved -- may then choose the family she/they prefer for the baby.

If you contact an adoption counselor, s/he will help you think through *your* situation. Even if you think you do want to release your baby for adoption, s/he will urge you to think carefully of all your alternatives before making your final decision.

LISA'S EXPERIENCE

Lisa, a lovely darkhaired senior, knew she wanted to go to college and have a career. Could she cope with motherhood at 17 and still carry through with her own plans? She decided to talk to a counselor at Children's Home Society, a large adoption agency. She relates her story:

> At first I almost didn't call Pat (the agency caseworker) because I thought someone from an adoption agency would want to talk to me just for my kid -- that she would try to con me into giving my baby up and signing the paper as fast as possible. I'd even heard adoption agencies referred to as baby-stealers! But she wasn't like that at all. . .

> Pat never did try to talk me into adoption -- she just wanted to help me find out what would be best for me.

> You see, I tried to ignore my pregnancy for at least six months. I didn't believe it at first -- I kept going to school and ignoring the whole thing. By four months I had to admit this had happened, but I told only two friends in the

next couple of months. I kept wearing my coat to
school so no one else would know. I was pretty
miserable.

Finally my parents found out. They were really understanding -- I had thought they would about
kill me, but instead my mother simply said, "Well,
we'll have to take you to the doctor tomorrow."

At first my mother assumed I was going to keep
the baby. But when I started talking to Pat, Mom
apparently thought it would be better for me to
give it up. She didn't say so, but I could tell
by the things she did say like "What are you going to do?" and "How will you support it?" I was
about a semester away from high school graduation
and I planned to go on to college.

I talked to Pat five or six times during
those last two months. Sometimes we would talk
for two or three hours about all kinds of things.
Of course we talked about adoption and what I
could do without a kid. I remember once I said I
didn't think hardly anyone who is real young
could make it with a baby. Pat told me that was
not so -- that for some people it's better to
keep the baby, and for others, to give it up.
She told me about different couples ready to adopt
a child, couples she thought might be right for my

baby if I decided on adoption.

I especially remember one couple -- the man was president of his company and the mother stayed home. They had a big house and several horses. That would have been nice for Stevie. Of course I know love is the most important thing, but I would have liked him to have money too.

When I was considering adoption, I worried that when he learned he was adopted, he might hate me for giving him up. It would be nice if, when you give your baby up for adoption, you could know that when he is 18, you could see him and explain to him yourself why you did it.

I had only one friend who thought I should release my baby. All the rest were against it. They would say, "Oh God, how could you?" and "Don't even say that, how could you think of giving it away?"

People in our class at school would talk about another girl who was giving up her baby. They said, "How can she do that after going through all that pain?" I told some of them it takes more love to give a baby up than it does to keep it!

A lot of girls don't consider adoption because they worry about what other people think. I thought about that, too. I did think about adoption, but never was sure what I wanted to do. Then when he was born, my mother brought me flowers. My friends came to see me and the baby. It would have been terribly hard to face them if I had decided to release him. It must be awful at that point for girls who do.

But I kept him and I'm glad I did. My mother helps me a lot, and my parents are willing to let me stay here while I go on to school.

I want to be a dental hygienist. They make pretty good money -- that's one of the things I

Like about it. But you can also pick your own hours. When I do get a job, I'll be able to be home when Stevie comes home from school. I'd like that because I could be here and watch him grow.

"Had you planned to be a dental hygienist before you became pregnant?"

I had thought about it a little, but I guess I had always wanted something better, like being a veterinarian. I might still go to school at night later when he's a little older. Perhaps I could become a dentist. But I know I'll enjoy being a dental hygienist.

"How has your life changed -- how is this summer with a four month old baby different from last summer?"

Just going to the beach! I used to take only my towel. Now I have a bassinet, diapers, food, sun shade, extra clothes. . .and I go only once or twice a week. (Last year I went every day!) I don't go by myself either because I need a little help carrying everything. But it's not that different. I do have to think ahead more -- I can't do things on the spur of the moment.

But it's kind of a nice change. The La Leche League speaker (organization for women who breast-feed their babies) at school said breastfeeding is nice for the mother because she *has* to sit down and relax when she feeds her baby. She can't prop a bottle, then go on working furious-ly. I agree -- and I'm enjoying relaxing with Stevie instead of always being on the go like I used to be.

I'm not dating right now -- I don't want to, perhaps because I'm pretty busy -- but I don't feel tied down with him. I can do just about anything I did before, so long as I include him in my plans.

It wasn't easy those first two months. When I first came home from the hospital, I thought

I'd die! He wet about every 15 minutes, and I'm
sure I didn't get even an hour's sleep those
first two nights. I thought, "How long will
this last?" Sometimes I thought about adoption
again because those first two months were terrible.

But when he was two months and one week old,
he started sleeping through the night. Now he
usually wakes about 6 a.m. I put him in bed
with me and nurse him. Then he goes back to
sleep.

ADOPTIVE FAMILIES SELECTED

Lisa's story matches the blurb in an agency brochure: "When you're pregnant and you're not married, it
often seems that everybody's trying to tell you what to do.
That's when Children's Home Society can help. We don't
want to take over your life or tell you what you should do.
We just want to help you make the best decisions possible
for yourself and your child."

Agencies, which may be public, voluntary, or sec-
tarian (church related), usually select their adoptive families very carefully. In fact, agencies have been highly
criticized for being *too* selective. But if it were your
baby they were placing, would you criticize their efforts
at finding the best family possible?

Families who apply for a healthy baby through an
agency must expect to wait at least two years, often longer. Children's Home Society of California will accept a
limited number of applications -- only enough to assure
sufficient approved adoptive homes to provide a good selection for the children they expect to place over a two
year period. Charlotte De Armond, State Director of
Public Affairs for CHS, explained, "We don't think it
helps anyone to have an extremely long list of people waiting to be considered as adoptive parents." The result of
this policy is that a high percentage of people applying for
consideration as adoptive parents never get into the system at all.

"The people we do consider are those who are so in-
sistent that they keep calling us," Ms. De Armond commented. "They ask if we're opening intake. Are we studying
families? The family who calls only once is not apt to be
considered. We're far more likely to investigate, then
place a child, with couples who are persistent."

Reason for this wait, of course, is that so few babies
are released for adoption. According to Ms. De Armond,
her agency gets twenty inquiries about adopting a healthy
infant for each baby that is available for adoption!

Prospective adoptive parents usually attend a group
meeting with other would-be parents. At this meeting they
learn about the children who are waiting for adoption. They
explore their own reasons for wanting to adopt a child.
They also learn more about the process of adoption. After
they have filled out a lengthy application form, an agency
social worker meets with them together and separately, and
visits them in their home. Topics discussed usually include
their reasons for wanting to adopt a child, the strength of

their marriage, their attitudes toward childrearing, their financial stability, and their capabilities for parenting a child born to someone else.

Basically, the agency is looking for the kind of parents you would like your child to have if you decide you want someone else to raise him/her. They want couples who have a stable home life where a child will fit in comfortably. Above all, they want a home where a child will feel wanted and loved.

JENNIFER'S DILEMMA

Jennifer had a special request concerning her baby's adoptive parents. In fact, she switched agencies because of that special request:

I knew right away I was pregnant because when I have a period I'm right on the dot. I started eating better for the baby's sake, but I thought I wanted to adopt because I knew I couldn't keep it -- not when I was only 14 and in the ninth grade.

For at least a month I didn't tell anybody. Then I told one friend that I was pregnant and was going to place the baby for adoption. She immediately said she would take it, but I said no. So she agreed it was my decision. During the next two or three months I told three other friends, and they didn't bug me -- just said it was up to me. Of course I thought about abortion, but I had always thought it was wrong so I didn't go that route.

By Christmas I started to show and everybody began talking around school and I just couldn't handle it. My mother still didn't know. So right after the holidays I talked with my counselor. I hadn't even gotten a pregnancy test yet and I was at least five months pregnant. She told me about the special class for pregnant students and urged me to get to the doctor *soon.*

So that same day I visited the class and went to the hospital for a pregnancy check. That night I told my mother. All she said was, "How could you?" Of course she was upset, but she took it pretty good. She didn't talk much for three days, but she did sign the necessary papers so I could enroll in the special class the next day. My new teacher thought I was quite efficient to get all that done in one day.

The class was fine except that some of the girls seemed to be against me because I was giving my baby up. Sometimes I felt so bad. The worst day was when a girl said, "Are you still giving your baby away?" I said I was, and she replied, "You're a fool!"

I was furious, so I said, "Don't you ever call me a fool!" At that point one of the teachers told the girls that she had adopted her son, and it had worked out fine. They liked her a lot, so after that they let me alone.

I've always been strong, but while I was pregnant, I couldn't handle things so well. I would really feel hurt. But some of the girls were understanding. They'd say, "It's your decision, so don't worry about what anyone else thinks."

I couldn't stand comments on the other side either. While I was in the doctor's office waiting to have my blood pressure checked, I heard one nurse say to another, "Is she giving it up for adoption?" When the other nurse said I was, the first one commented, "That's good. She's too young -- she shouldn't keep it." I suppose I'm stubborn -- but at that point I felt more like keeping the baby than at any other time!

First I talked to a counselor from a big agency. But my mother wanted to be sure the baby was placed with a family with the same religion as ours. The first caseworker said she would try, but she couldn't promise. Then my Mom heard about a smaller agency, one that works only with Christian families. Their social worker said they did have a family waiting who belonged to a church like ours.

After I delivered, one nurse was especially nice to me. She got her baby through adoption, and she would come in and talk to me. When I was in labor, we got really close. She invited me over to her house, and I think I'll be baby-sitting for her. Her daughter is five years old now and she really loves her.

My baby was born after several hours of very hard labor. I didn't see him -- I had decided earlier that I didn't want to. If I did I might want him. But my Mom and all my friends saw him. He has brown hair and blue eyes, they said.

I wrote him a letter and sent him a little gift. The social worker said she would get it to him.

"How would you feel if your baby tried to find you later?"

I don't know how I'd react. I probably would be happy that he would want to know who I am. But I suppose it would depend partly on how much I've told my husband and other kids. I'd like to know he's OK.

I wouldn't go searching though. If he wants to find me, fine, but I won't go out and look. That could be hard on him. . .all of a sudden to have me pop up and say, "Hello, I'm your mother!"

I'm glad I did it this way. But I do think about him. I was thinking this morning that next month he'll be two years old. It's getting easier as time goes by.

"Any advice for other 14-year-olds?"

Well, a 14-year-old isn't ready to be a mother -- she's still growing up herself. Janeen

the time when release of names may be lawful.

Birth parents can sometimes keep in touch with the adoptive family through the agency caseworker. Birth parents occasionally write to their worker, perhaps years later, with information to share with their child. Adoptive parents can also give the caseworker information about their child to share with the birth parents.

Recently an agency in California granted the request of a 15 year old father and a 16 year old mother to meet the people who were to adopt their child. After the meeting they felt so good about the situation that they set up a plan with the social worker. Each year on the child's birthday they will send an update on their lives to the social worker. The adoptive family will do the same. The social worker will then see that each gets the others' report.

Reuben Pannor, co-author of *The Adoption Triangle* (Anchor Press/Doubleday: 1978) and director of social work and research at Vista Del Mar Child Care Service in Los Angeles, reports that his agency is satisfying similar requests. Occasionally a birth parent meets the adoptive parents before they relinquish their child through Vista Del Mar.

Perhaps you know you don't want to "give your baby to strangers," but you might be interested in adoption if you could meet the adoptive parents. You'd like to satisfy yourself that they are the kind of people you want to parent your child. Discuss your thinking with your caseworker. If that agency doesn't permit such a plan yet, perhaps another agency in your area will.

Meeting the adoptive parents does not, of course, change the finality of actual relinquishment. "Relinquishment" means a legal document has been signed by the birth parents. This document has been accepted by a representative of the adoption agency which has agreed to take the child for placement. At this time the agency takes over the responsibility for the care of the child until it is placed with an adoptive family.

Relinquishment becomes "final and binding" (you

can't change your mind about giving up your child) when
these signed papers are filed by the agency with the State
Department of Social Services. Once the birth parents have
signed the relinquishment papers and the relinquishment has
been accepted by the State Department of Social Services,
they generally no longer have any legal rights or responsibility for their child.

Some groups across the country are working toward
a change in this current law, however. Some would like
birth parents to have an interval of time in which they could
decide to keep their child even after they have signed the relinquishment papers.

At this time, relinquishment papers can never be
signed by the mother until after delivery, usually after she
leaves the hospital. She signs a *release* form while she is
in the hospital stating that someone else (the agency representative if it is an agency adoption) can take the baby away
from the hospital. This does *not* mean the birth mother or
father has signed away her/his rights to the child.

As soon as the birth mother and father have signed
the relinquishment papers, the baby can be placed in its permanent adoptive home. S/he will be in a foster home until
these papers are completed. Sometimes, if both the birth
mother and father have made their decision immediately after
birth, the father can sign at once and the mother can complete this step on her way home from the hospital. If this
happens, their baby can probably be placed immediately with
the adoptive family, a nice situation for a new baby.

Not all states have the same laws regarding adoption,
however. A Uniform Adoption Act has been accepted by some
states but not all. If you decide to place your baby through
an adoption agency, the agency worker will make a point of
informing you of all the rights you have under the law in your
state.

JODIE'S DECISION

Jodie assumed she would keep her child. But, when
she was about six months pregnant, she began thinking more
and more about the realities of mothering, of the tremendous

changes a baby would bring into her life:

Jodie was president of the youth group at her church, an eleventh grader everyone looked up to. If anyone else had a problem, her pastor would say, "Go see Jodie."

She was 16 and dating a 20-year-old. They had sex only once. Two weeks later in late April she told Tim she thought she was pregnant. Her periods had always been completely regular, but he told her she was just worried. . .that of course she wasn't pregnant after only one time!

A week or two later she told him again, and once more he assured her it was just because she was worried about it, and that she really wasn't pregnant.

When they realized she was, he said, "I'll do whatever you want -- pay for an abortion, marry you. . ." But her feelings made abortion an impossible choice at that time. As for marriage. . . it didn't seem a good solution. In fact, Jodie wasn't seeing much of Tim during those weeks.

Summer came, school was out, and she had told no one else. This simply couldn't happen to Jodie.

Then her best friend came to her for counseling. She and her boy friend were very close and it was getting more and more difficult not to "go all the way." Did Jodie really think it would be a sin if they had sex? After all, they loved each other, and what harm would there be? What risks?

"I urged her not to. . .hinted at great risk. She didn't seem to hear me, didn't really think I knew what I was talking about," Jodie explained. "Finally I simply told her. . .told her I had been that route and that I was pregnant. She didn't believe me at first."

But this friend was her only confidant. Jodie was still president of the group at church. She continued her other activities there. Her "long hot summer" dragged by.

Should she go to the church retreat in the mountains in August? She would be at least five months pregnant by then. "I wished I could confide in my mother. But how could I hurt her?" she pondered. "I kept thinking, if she would only ask, simply say, 'Jodie, are you pregnant?' but she didn't."

Jodie went to the mountain retreat. She found something there:

"I found God as I never had before. I felt this terrific peace come over me. I suddenly realized my problems would be worked out. I still had no idea how, but I knew my life would somehow be OK."

She went home. The two girls who had gone to camp with her had never realized she was pregnant. No one at home seemed to have the slightest inkling. But finally her mother said, "Jodie, I'm taking you to the doctor. We have got to find out why you haven't had a period for so long."

"I was so relieved," Jodie remembers. "Finally she would know. But I still didn't tell her until I came out of the doctor's office. Then I could finally say, 'Mom, I'm pregnant.'"

Her mother's first reaction was, "Where did I go wrong?" Her next, "What will you do?"

Tim came over. The family talked about various possibilities. Was marriage the solution? Marriage would at least help the situation as far as the church and, perhaps, their own faith was concerned. But both Jodie and Tim realized a pregnancy was not enough reason for a long-time commitment. An aunt suggested marriage followed by a quick annulment "so the baby would have a name." Jodie couldn't see the value of "a name."

Jodie's senior year in high school would soon start. She thought about her school and her friends

there. She wasn't about to join the yearly army
of young girls who drop out of school because of
pregnancy. But neither did she want to go back to
her scheduled classes, to the counselor who had
taken such a special interest in her college plans,
the physical education teacher who had been so
proud of her outstanding basketball record. She
could go to Colorado, hide at her aunt's home for
the duration. But hiding in Colorado didn't seem
a solution. She would have to. . .want to. . .
come back home some time.

Her sister told her of the special class for
pregnant students in her school district. She
called the teacher the Friday before school started. The next day, a wet and dreary September Saturday (most September Saturdays in California are
warm and bright. . .what happened today?) the
teacher visited Jodie and her mother. She explained the special program, and pointed out that
Jodie could continue her academic studies -- her
Civics, writing a research paper for Senior English. In addition, she could learn prepared
childbirth techniques in the adaptive physical
education class. (Childbirth takes as much condi-
tioning and stamina as does starring in a basketball game, she was reminded.) She would have a
chance to discuss the options available to herself
and other pregnant teenagers.

Jodie and her mother implied that Jodie would
keep the baby, that adoption was not an option
they were considering at that time. "Although I
certainly will back Jodie in whatever decision she
makes," her mother assured the teacher.

Jodie enrolled in the school Monday. She
got along well with the other girls, performed
well academically, and found plenty of time (too
much, according to her teacher!) to talk with
other students.

Two counselors from a youth counseling service volunteered each week to lead a rap session in the class. Emphasis was on learning to understand oneself and mention was seldom made of decision-making in regard to marriage vs. single motherhood vs. adoption. Jodie occasionally commented that she didn't know what she would do when the baby was born, but she didn't really want to talk to another counselor.

The "on call" adoption agency counselor had been in class with her film, "I'm 17, I'm Pregnant, and I Don't Know What to Do." The film tells the story of a 17-year-old who kept her baby, then after 14 months found she couldn't cope, so relinquished her son for adoption -- a real tear-jerker of a film.

The teacher asked Jodie several times that fall if she would like to talk to Pat from the agency (and Pat asked the teacher lots of times!) -- but each time Jodie said, "No, not yet."

(Pat was getting nervous because she knew, if Jodie had not yet made her decision to keep or to relinquish, she needed time to think through her

DO I WANT TO BE A PARENT?

options. If she kept her baby, she would have a
lot of preparation before the baby was born. If
she decided to relinquish, she needed time to
choose the "right" family. And Tim would have to
be involved in a relinquishment decision.)

Finally, in early November, Jodie consented
to see Pat. They talked a number of times. As
Jodie considered her options, relinquishment
seemed the best course. After more discussion,
Tim also agreed to sign the relinquishment papers.

The baby was due in early December.

Jodie had worked with her teacher to complete
most of her semester's course work by the time she
delivered because they agreed she might not want
to come back to the special class after delivery
-- without her baby. It could be difficult to
face all the others, each of whom was planning
at that time to keep her child.

By the first week in December, she was
ready. Most of her work was done. She still had
her research paper to write, but she had completed the preliminaries, and she knew she could do
that at home after delivery.

The week went by. . .and the next week
dragged on with nothing but a few false labor contractions. Pat was leaving for the Christmas holidays so she gave Jodie another social worker's
phone number. By the end of the third week, Pat
had flown back to Kansas City with her family.

Jodie was feeling -- and looking -- very
large, rather tired, and eager for this whole
thing to be over. Not that it would ever be over, exactly -- she knew this experience would be
in her memory forever, but. . .well, she was
ready for it to be in her memory, not her body!

School was out for the Christmas holidays on
December 17. Saturday and Sunday seemed inter-
minable as Jodie tried to get into the spirit of

preparing for Christmas with her mother and little
sister.

Sunday was especially hard. She hadn't gone
to her church since November. One of the women
had told her mother she didn't think Jodie should
go to worship after she "showed." Jodie was hurt,
and says now that she most needed her church then.
But she cared about other people's feelings enough
to go along with this viewpoint.

Monday. . .then Tuesday, and still no baby.
By Wednesday morning, the contractions started.
The doctor said she would have the baby by evening
. . .but it was 24 hours before her son was finally
born -- December 23, three weeks later than expected.

It didn't occur to Jodie that day or the next
to phone Joyce, the social worker whose phone number
Pat had given her. She was too tired to think of
much of anything.

Saturday -- Christmas morning. . .Jodie's doctor told her she could go home if she liked, that
Christmas Day was reason enough to leave a day early.

But what about the baby? She suddenly realized
nothing had been finalized.

She frantically called Joyce. . .no answer.
Jodie had had Pat's home number for a month, but only Joyce's office number. No one answered. (Adoption agency people celebrate Christmas too.)

What could she do? She didn't want to spend
Christmas Day in the hospital.

The hospital would not keep the baby without
the mother. The only solution was to take the
baby home with her.

The house was full of relatives. Jodie was
tired. She hadn't been around infants much, and she
hadn't been involved in the baby care classes at
school or in the hospital. She had ignored them because she wasn't keeping her baby. But she managed

that day with her mother's help. She called Joyce
the next day, but still no answer. Could it be
she wasn't "meant" to give up her baby? She was
beginning to wonder.

Next morning her mother went off to work. A
little later, Jodie dialed Joyce's number again.

"Children's Home Society. To whom do you
wish to speak?"

"Joyce Smith, please."

"Just a minute. I'll ring her office."

"Hello, this is Joyce."

Two hours later Joyce picked up the baby.
Jodie and Tim signed the final papers a few days
later, and the baby was placed with the couple
she and Pat had selected.

Jodie went back to her high school for her
last semester, graduated with her class, and went
on to college as she had planned.

She also returned to her church soon after
she had relinquished her baby. A few months later she was asked to lead a group of junior high
girls. She became more and more active in her
church. Occasionally she shares with her junior
high group and others her experiences with her
baby.

When someone has a problem, the minister often says, "Go see Jodie. . ."

RONDA: PREGNANT AGAIN

A lot of teenagers who have had one child have another within one or two years. A study reported by the
United States Department of Health, Education, and Welfare (October, 1979) states that 44 percent of teenage mothers are pregnant again within a year after the first birth,
and 70 percent pregnant within the second year.

Girls who remain in school, however, have a much

lower rate of repeat pregnancies. But it does happen.

Ronda dropped by school one rainy February afternoon with her announcement. John, $1\frac{1}{2}$, was with her:

I'm pregnant again. . .but I'm going to give it
up for adoption.

"What about Dennis?"

We split two months ago -- before I knew I was
pregnant. When I called him to tell him I was, he
was very upset. I've already called Pat, and we
have an appointment with her next week.

I had trouble taking the pill. I tried several kinds, and I was on it when I got pregnant this
second time. In fact, I went to the doctor to re-
new my prescription, and after he examined me, he
told me I was two months pregnant!

I haven't considered an abortion. I figure
the baby has a right to live and I don't have a
right to take that life. Somebody else who can't
have kids should have him (or her). So I decided
on adoption almost right away. I figure I have
enough with John, that I have my hands full. I
know all three of us, John, the new baby, and I
will be better off if I give him up.

Ronda returned a few months later to continue her
story:

You remember I had that appointment with Pat?
I thought Dennis would go with me, but he didn't.
Then Pat wanted to talk to him, and after that he
decided he wanted custody. He didn't change his
mind about relinquishment until two weeks after
Seth was born. Seth was in foster care during that
time.

I took care of Seth while we were in the hospital -- fed him and diapered him. The nurses
kept trying to talk me out of adoption. They had
been there when I had John, so they were surprised
that I was giving this one up. They had their own

opinions, but I didn't think it was any of their business.

A friend of mine took a picture of Seth while he was in the nursery. Of course I still have it.

I never met Seth's family. They're outdoor people -- like to camp and fish -- and they're into athletics. It was important to Dennis that our son have a chance to camp, play ball, and do all those things that Dennis enjoys so much.

"What could you say to a 15-year-old who is pregnant, something that might help her with her decisions?"

Each person is different -- I suppose I would tell her to do what she thinks is best for her and her baby, not what someone else thinks would be best for them. You get to feeling closed in sometimes. My mother offered to help with John at first, but I just took him all to myself. This made it hard when I first came home. If there is someone to help, let them. My Mom used to tell me, "You go out and I'll take care of him," but I wouldn't do it. I'd stay with him -- and you know how frustrated I got.

I think about Seth all the time, but it doesn't bother me. I know it was better for him, better for me, and better for John. John takes up all my time, and I feel if Seth has a family of his own, he'll get that much more love and attention.

———

Adoptive parents pay fees covering a portion of the cost of counseling services to them both before and after adoption. Fees are usually on a sliding scale based on the adoptive couple's income. The maximum fee covers services to the family and the child after the placement has been made. An agency cannot provide financial assistance to the birth mother, but the social worker should be able to refer you to others who will give you the help you need.

If you do decide on adoption, the agency will take care of all the legal aspects. They stay abreast of new legislation and are very aware of *your* needs. They want whatever is best for you.

Doctors and lawyers often consider the adoptive family to be their primary client. If they do, they may not act in your best interest because they are thinking first of the adoptive family.

FOSTER CARE

Ronda mentioned that Seth had had *foster* care for a short period of time before he went to his adoptive parents' home. He didn't go to his permanent home until after his father had signed the relinquishment papers.

A foster family takes care of children on a short-term basis. The child's parents keep legal custody of him/her.

Sometimes foster care is used by a mother who has not decided whether she wants to keep her baby or place him for adoption. She may request that the baby be placed in a foster home while she makes up her mind.

This can be a good approach if you know you haven't made a firm decision when the baby is born. Perhaps all you need are two or three weeks to think through your situation. And you may realize that if you take the baby home with you, you probably couldn't bear to give her up later -- even if your head told you that would be best for both of you.

Although foster care is meant for short-term situations like this, it is often misused. Many children in the United States have been placed in foster care, left there for a long time, years in some cases, while their parents try to "pull themselves together." In the meantime, the child may be shifted from one foster home to another, never having the love and caring that a permanent family could give him. This is very hard on a child.

The child in foster care keeps his own name. Foster parents are paid the cost of clothes, room, and board. If the placement is voluntary, the child's parent may return at any time, or the child may be transferred to another foster home.

The foster mother, although she may be warm and caring, must not allow herself to love the child as if he were her own because he could be -- and often is -- taken away after a short (or long) period of time.

Children need "real" parenting, whether from birth parents or adoptive parents. Foster care can provide short-term help, but for the sake of the child, it should never be considered a long-term solution to the possible problems of caring for your child yourself.

CHAPTER 4

Independent Adoption

Birth parents often choose *independent* adoption if they want to pick out their baby's adoptive family. Parents who relinquish to an agency usually have some choice in the selection of the adoptive family for their baby. But they may want to be even more involved in the process. . .or they may have requests which the agency can't handle.

Independent adoption means an adoption in which the birth parents select the adoptive family. They place their child directly with that family. A few states don't allow independent placement of children, but most do.

To make the placement legal, the birth parents sign a "consent to adoption." This names the specific couple with whom their child is placed. This consent must be signed in the presence of a representative of the State Department of Social Services or its local designee.

The lawyer can take consent from the birth parents to place the child with the prospective adoptive family. This is termed the "Take into care" form and is not the final adoption paper.

If birth parents decide to "go independent," it is important that they consult a reputable lawyer. When birth parents relinquish to an agency, the agency takes care of all the legal matters for them. In an independent adoption, they are *on their own*. Legal help is essential whether the baby goes to relatives or to strangers.

In actual practice, the birth parents frequently do not know the family which adopts their baby. Sometimes a girl's doctor "knows someone." Or she may go to a lawyer who specializes in adoption services. The lawyer may have several, perhaps many, clients who wish to adopt a baby. He may tell the girl about one or more families and suggest she make the choice.

Usually a baby who is independently placed will go home from the hospital with its new family. In most states, the adoptive family is not studied to determine its fitness to adopt the child until *after the baby is already in their home.*

At that time, after they already have the child, the couple files an adoption petition in court. Then the state agency must study them to decide if they are fit to have this baby. Will they love him and provide a good family life for him? Is the child suitable for this particular family? The state agency also interviews the birth parents to learn about family background, medical history, etc. This information is given to the adoptive family to share with the child.

The birth mother may, as soon as she leaves the hospital after delivery, sign papers relinquishing her child to an adoption agency. However, she (and the father) may not sign for independent adoption until after information about the home study of the adoptive parents is shared with them.

At this time she (they) sign the consent to adoption. This usually happens about six weeks to two months after the baby has been placed with the adoptive family. Up until that time, either the birth parents or the adoptive parents are free to change their minds about the adoption agreement. If there is no legal paperwork stating otherwise, the birth parent is responsible for consenting for medical care during this interval.

NOTE: If a baby leaves the hospital with anyone other than its birth mother, the hospital will require the birth mother to sign a release form. This does *not* mean the baby is released for adoption! It simply means the baby may be taken from the hospital by someone other than its birth parent. If the baby's mother, for example, has to stay in the hospital for an extra day, her own mother may take her baby home. The infant's mother would have to sign this release form before the baby could leave with its grandmother.

The hospital release form means the same thing whether the baby is released to its grandmother, to an adoption agency, or to adoptive parents. In each situation, the birth parent still has all parental rights.

As soon as the birth parents have signed the consent to adoption, however, they can change their minds only if the court agrees the withdrawal of consent is "in the child's best interest." When the adoption is final (which takes about six months in many states), the birth parents no longer have a right to ask for the return of their child.

ANNE MEETS ADOPTIVE PARENTS

Anne chose independent adoption. She's glad she did because in her case this meant meeting her baby's adoptive parents before delivery. Knowing they were "nice" people was reassuring.

Two weeks after her fourteenth birthday she suspected she was pregnant. She pushed the idea out of her mind, however, and did nothing about it for nearly five months. Her boy friend finally insisted on taking her to the clinic for a pregnancy test:

I thought at the time I could get an abortion. The doctor didn't tell me what to do, didn't examine me. He just referred me to someone else. Next morning I decided I had to tell my Mom because I couldn't do that (get an abortion) all by myself. So I got up, woke my Mom, and told her. It was kind of sad.

She took me to our doctor that same day and

he told us I was too far along -- it would be
illegal to get an abortion here in California.
But he said I could fly to New York and get one
there. But that would have had to be a saline
abortion and I didn't want that.

So he asked if I was interested in adoption.
He told us about independent adoption and said
he knew someone who could help us if that's what
we wanted. That's when I first started thinking
about adoption. Until that visit I assumed I
would have an abortion.

I didn't go back to my regular school after
that. My Mom knew about the special school for
pregnant girls and she called the teacher. The
next week was spring vacation so I had some time
to think. I enrolled the following Monday. By
then my whole school knew I was pregnant.

"Did you get much flack at school?"

No, I really didn't. But by the time I enrolled in the special school, I figured I was
going to place the baby for adoption. I guess
my parents did influence my thinking, but I remember agreeing that adoption was the best
thing. Of course I thought about it a lot. I
knew I didn't have to, that being young doesn't
stop a lot of people from keeping the baby. But
that wasn't what I wanted.

The other pregnant girls would sometimes
say, "Well, I certainly would never give my baby up." Most of them were against adoption, although I think one or two were kind of leaning
toward it. It didn't bother me too much. Of
course I was sad that I wasn't going to have a
baby and everyone else in the class was. But I
still realized what would happen and I knew what
I wanted. The teacher sometimes showed films
and held discussions about what really happens
if you're in high school and are trying to take
care of a baby too -- or if you drop out of

school. I *knew* I didn't want that!

"You always seemed very secure in your choice. Why do you suppose you made this decision?"

Perhaps the way I was raised. My parents didn't push me but they thought adoption was a good idea. A lot of the girls in the class wanted to get married (because of pregnancy), but I didn't even think of that.

After I decided I wanted to go through independent adoption, my parents called a lawyer. When I was about seven months pregnant, she (my lawyer) showed me the file on the couple who were to adopt my baby. I read the whole thing -- it told their histories, where they lived, what kind of work they did, etc. Then my lawyer gave them my phone number, and two or three weeks later they called to ask if they could come over to meet me. Of course we wanted them to. They came that Sunday. My parents were here, and they all talked a lot. The couple was *so* nice, and they made me feel about one hundred times better about the whole thing. I knew then that my baby would have the kind of parents I wanted for him.

I saw my baby when he was born, and before I left the hospital I visited him in the nursery. One nurse bothered me. She told me, "Well, if it was up to me, I wouldn't let you see it." That made me mad because it was none of her business. Another nurse, though, was especially nice. She talked to me a lot -- told me that she had had a baby when she was 16. I appreciated her, because it is those first few hours and days that are the hardest when you give up your baby.

For the first two weeks after I had him I was really wondering about adoption. But what it really comes down to is it doesn't matter how I felt -- you have to think about the baby and how he'll have a better life with someone else.

"Do you think about him often?"

Well, yes, I think about him, but I don't *worry* about him. I've put it all behind me, but I certainly haven't forgotten about him.

"So much is being said and written now about 'open records' -- the idea that some adoptees want very much to find their birth parents but often can't. Their birth records were sealed when they were adopted and can't be released on request in most states. Your baby's parents have met you, and your child can find you later if he likes. Does the idea bother you?"

Not at all. I have always thought in the back of my head that maybe I'll meet him some time. Perhaps I'll go looking for him but I probably won't go up and tell him. They asked me when I signed the final papers if it would be all right if he looked for me. Of course I said that would be fine.

I can understand why some adoptive parents would worry that if there is no secrecy, the birth mother might come back and want the baby. But I think they would also like to see where their baby is coming from. My son's parents told me they were glad they had met me.

"If a pregnant 14-year-old asked you for advice, what would you tell her?"

I would say you have to think about it a lot before you make any kind of decision at all. You have to consider yourself and you have to consider the baby. You have to remember that the baby has to come before yourself.

The way I look at it is -- if you give a baby up for adoption, you're making an accident that could be bad into something really good. You're giving something wonderful to someone else. I know I made those two people very happy. I know I don't have guilt feelings about *that!*

(friend who has a baby) cracks me up. She just
turned 14 and she's going to keep it! But she's
going to want to go out just as I did. And she's
going to be leaving that baby with her mother a
lot -- or staying home.

I want to do so much -- go to college and do
something with my life. I want to grow up slowly -- I didn't want suddenly to have to be mature.
I wanted to take my time. And a baby wouldn't
have fit in. Janeen will have to grow up quickly
because a child needs a mother to look up to. She
can't be playing games while the baby is, too.
She'll have to be more mature.

I'm content with my decision.

QUESTION OF SECRECY

Jennifer completed the form for her baby's birth certificate while she was in the hospital. After the adoption was
finalized, a new birth certificate was issued. In this one,
the adoptive parents were listed as if the baby had been born
to them. The first birth certificate, the one with Jennifer's
and the baby's biological father's names on it, will be
"sealed" -- filed away where it cannot be seen except by
order of the court.

Secrecy traditionally has been an important part of
agency adoptions. If birth parents wanted to meet the adoptive parents, they could choose independent adoption. Many
people, however, prefer to go through an agency because of
the careful checking they do with the adoptive families and
because of the counseling they offer the birth parents. The
agency acts as the birth parents' advocate.

Recently agency workers have been asking birth parents if they want their names released to their child if s/he
requests them when s/he is an adult.

In most states at this time, the law won't allow release of these names if the adoption occurred through an
agency. Because there is a movement to change the law,
agencies are asking for this permission in preparation for

LAWYER'S ROLE

Anne mentioned "her" lawyer. She and her parents hired a lawyer to represent *them*. Her baby's adoptive parents were represented by a different lawyer. This is much better than having one lawyer represent both birth and adoptive parents.

If one lawyer handles the entire case, a lawyer hired by the adoptive parents, she may not act in the best interests of the birth parents. If the birth mother, for example, considers changing her mind and keeping her child, the adoptive parents' lawyer would tend to think first of the rights and wishes of her primary clients, the adoptive parents. She might even attempt to talk the young mother into giving up her baby against her wishes.

In California, more infants are placed for adoption independently than through agencies, according to David Leavitt. Leavitt is an attorney in Beverly Hills, California, whose entire practice consists of handling independent adoption cases. He places about 200 babies each year, about the same number of infants as are placed annually through the entire Los Angeles County Department of Adoptions. During the past 19 years Leavitt has placed about 1250 babies in adoptive homes. More than 1100 birth mothers of these babies met "their" adoptive parents.

"When couples come in telling me they want to adopt a baby," Leavitt explained, "they fill out a rather complete questionnaire first. Then I talk with them for at least two hours. In that time I can spot dingalings -- and if I do, I turn them away. But most people who want to adopt are pretty good people."

"How do you decide who gets which baby?" I asked.

"Many of my clients find their own babies," he answered. "During that first interview I tell them how to go about finding an adoptable infant. I suggest they make out a resume complete with their picture, reasons they want to adopt, their income, profession, where they live, etc. Obstetricians are the best sources for information about an adoptable baby. So I advise them to get that resume to as many obstetricians as possible. Many of them come back later with information about a baby who, when born, will be available for adoption."

Because state law in California declares that the independent adoption is a placement by the birth parents to the adoptive parents, strict interpretation of the law would allow the lawyer *only* to perform necessary legal services for the baby's two sets of parents. Those who follow this interpretation believe he should not "match" babies and adoptive families.

In actual practice, however, couples who want to adopt a child frequently ask a lawyer or obstetrician, sometimes their minister, if they know of "available" children. A young woman who is unhappily pregnant may ask her doctor what she can do. Or her doctor may ask her if she is interested in placing for adoption.

When a prospective birth mother approaches Leavitt, he talks to her, learns something about her and her wishes for her child. He then chooses from among his clients a family he thinks would be appropriate. He hands the young woman a file containing information about the couple. Usually a photograph is included. Almost always, he says, she agrees to the first family he picks.

Leavitt likes to speak of an adoption as a marriage between the baby and its adoptive parents. "I treat the young birth mother as the father of the bride," he said. "If I do my job properly, she will know all about that family and she will feel good about them parenting her baby."

After the selection is made (but before the baby is born), the adoptive parents are notified. They then telephone the young woman to ask if they can meet her. Usually, according to Leavitt, they meet at a restaurant for dessert and coffee. Often both the adoptive parents and the birth mother are reassured by this meeting.

When the baby is born, the adoptive parents generally send flowers to its mother, Leavitt said. "After all, she's the mother of their baby and they love her," he commented.

Leavitt's last contact with the young woman is usually in the hospital the day after she delivers her baby. The adoptive parents take the baby home from the hospital. Consent to adoption, as stated above, is not signed until the state agency has checked out the family.

Cost of adopting a baby through Leavitt varies between $3000 and $5000. His fee, he says, is $1250. The rest of the money is spent on the young mother's medical and hospital bills, sometimes also for her living expenses during pregnancy.

A criticism sometimes leveled at independent adoption is that, because the adoptive parents pay at least the birth mother's medical bills, she would have trouble changing her mind about the adoption. Even though she doesn't sign the consent to adopt until about six weeks after delivery, she might find it difficult to back out of such an arrangement. Leavitt insists this is not a problem. She has no legal obligation to repay these expenses. However, Leavitt did say that if she changes her mind and keeps her baby, her parents are apt to reimburse the adoptive family for the money spent on their daughter's medical care.

It is absolutely illegal for prospective adoptive parents to give the birth mother money strictly as a gift. Whatever she receives to pay medical bills and possibly her living expenses during pregnancy must be reported to the court.

If you are ever approached by someone who wants to pay you to let them adopt your child, you should report that person to the authorities immediately!

"It is lawful for the adoptive parents to pay for prenatal care and hospital stay. But you must file a statement when you adopt that you have paid only pregnancy costs and lawyer/agency fees. The law has always permitted this. If something more is added to 'sweeten the pot,' it's illegal," explained Nordin F. Blacker, attorney in San Jose, California. "This does cause complications if the birth mother changes her mind and keeps her baby after someone else has paid her fees," he added.

The birth mother can never give her consent to adopt

directly to the adoptive parents, to the doctor, or to the
lawyer. She must give that consent to the social worker
who represents the state. Before she signs that consent,
the social worker will tell her about the adoptive parents.
If she doesn't like what she hears, she can request that her
baby be returned to her. At that time she can still relinquish to an adoption agency if she wishes. According to
Leavitt, this almost never happens.

One young woman I interviewed had been told by her
doctor that her baby's adoptive father was a lawyer. She
had also assumed the mother would stay home to care for
her infant. It wasn't until after the home study had been
done that she learned the father was really a free lance
photographer employed only part-time. She also learned
the mother was a nurse working in the hospital where the
baby was delivered.

She felt cheated. But she didn't consider taking her
child back. He had been with his adoptive parents two
months and it didn't make sense to his birth mother to take
him from the parents he had already learned to love. But
she was frustrated at being deceived.

Her frustration could, perhaps, have been prevented
if she had asked more questions in the beginning. If you
release a child for independent adoption, you know there is
no agency doing a thorough check on your baby's future
family. So you have not only a right, but also a responsibility to be as sure as you can be that the couple receiving
your baby are the kind of people *you* want to parent your
child.

Anne was delighted to meet her baby's adoptive parents. In most adoptions Leavitt handles, this occurs.
With independent adoption, even if the two sets of parents
don't meet, the names of each are on the consent to adoption paper. This, of course, means secrecy is not part of
the arrangement.

For some adoptive parents, this is a serious worry.
One adoptive mother mentioned she tried never to have her
two adopted children out of her sight during the early years
because she knew their birth mother knew where they lived.

She was afraid that, even though both adoptions had been legal and final, a birth parent might still attempt to retrieve her child. Such cases are occasionally mentioned in the papers or on television. In actual practice, it seldom happens.

An unskilled lawyer may cause problems. A student who released her child at birth thought the adoption was final. But six weeks later she learned she must fly across the country (at the adoptive parents' expense) to sign the final papers. She felt tricked.

Lack of secrecy can also be awkward for the birth mother. When one girl learned her baby was placed not far from her own neighborhood, she was concerned. Many of her friends didn't know about her pregnancy. Besides, she thought it would be hard to wonder if each child she met on the street might be "hers."

So the openness of independent adoption can work both ways. For some, it's great. For others, it's a worry.

But the biggest criticism of independent adoption is the lack of counseling usually available. Leavitt, for example, assumes his clients know that they want to release for adoption when they come into his office. A study of birth parents who had released for adoption independently is reported in *Adoptions Without Agencies: A Study of Independent Adoptions* by Meezan, Katz, and Russo (1978). Two-thirds of the 115 women interviewed reported that during pregnancy they had doubts about releasing their children for adoption. Less than half of these women discussed their doubts with the person arranging the adoption.

Most (85 percent) said they would have liked to talk to someone about their decision to surrender or about other personal problems. Only about one-fourth of them did discuss their concerns with someone trained to counsel persons under stress. Apparently they weren't given help in thinking about their options or in discussing other problems.

This lack of counseling can be a serious risk in independent adoption.

Birth parents who participated in a Children's Home Society of California survey ("The Changing Face of

Adoption," 1977) were asked, "Looking back today, do you
feel you made the right decision? Why or why not?" Almost
two-thirds of the 106 respondents replied that they had made
the right decision. CHS then analyzed the difference between those who felt they were right in relinquishing and
those who wished they had not.

The majority of those who thought they made the
right decision had felt no pressure from others to relinquish, *had received counseling,* and considered that
counseling very helpful. In addition, they had made their
own decisions to release the baby for adoption.

Research reported in *Adoptions Without Agencies*
suggests that most attorneys who handle adoption cases do
so only occasionally. The study reported that lawyers with
larger adoption practices tended to discuss alternatives and
refer to agencies more often than do those who handle only
an occasional adoption. The lawyers who placed babies
more often also tended to collect more background information on the birth parents. This may mean less risk to the
birth mother (and the adoptive parents) who "go independent" if they work with a lawyer with more experience in
adoption cases.

You might choose independent adoption because you
want to meet your baby's future parents. You may also
want to know your baby will go home with them directly
from the hospital. But you need to realize the risks in the
lack of counseling for you and in the lack of a home study
of the adoptive parents *before* they receive your child.

Independent adoption laws vary a great deal from
state to state. A few states do not permit independent adoption at all. One chapter in *Adoptions Without Agencies*
deals with the law on adoptive placement in each state. It
is also an excellent resource for learning more about independent adoption because of the extensive research reported.

If you do consider independent adoption, *be sure*
to contact a reputable lawyer for advice. If you adopt
through an agency, they will handle the legal matters. *In
an independent adoption, it's up to you.*

CHAPTER 5

Sometimes Relatives Adopt

Some young mothers -- about 2.5 percent of all pregnant teenagers, five percent of unmarried teens -- place their babies with relatives or friends who then raise the child. If this placement is legalized as an adoption, it is considered one kind of independent adoption.

Rosa came to southern California from Kansas to live with her older cousin and his wife during her pregnancy. Her friends in Kansas never knew she was pregnant. Her cousin and his wife already had three preschoolers, but they agreed to take her baby when they first learned she was pregnant.

Luckily for her plans, her baby was due in August. She managed to conceal the fact of her pregnancy until school was out. She flew immediately to California where she stayed until two weeks after her baby was born. Then she flew home and enrolled in her junior year of high school.

Rosa seems satisfied with the situation. She doesn't have the responsibility of parenting her child, but she does know where he is and how he is getting along.

For some birth parents, this can be a bad decision. Seeing her baby reared by someone else can be hard on the birth mother, even if, perhaps because, she is close to that person. She may decide three or four years later that she should be raising her "own" child, but finds that her baby's

adoptive parents, although related to her, aren't willing to
give up the child they consider their own.

One young woman who sent her baby to live with her
sister in another state said, "When Jennie is old enough to
understand, I'll ask her if she would rather live with me or
with my sister." But this would probably be unfair to the
child as well as to the adoptive (or foster) parents. A child
who lives with one set of parents for several years -- or
even one year --usually considers those parents to be the
"real" parents. Being asked to choose between them and
someone else who considers herself his "real" mother can
be devastating.

Sometimes, however, relative adoption works beautifully:

LYNN'S STORY

Lynn called me at school one chilly November day.
"Will you tell me about your class?" she asked.

Two hours later I was talking with her and her
mother in their comfortable, upper middleclass home. Her
mother was busily preparing a turkey for roasting. She
explained they were taking it with them the next evening on
a Thanksgiving weekend camping trip. Several brothers
and sisters came in and out as we talked. Lynn's father
appeared briefly. He had recently started a printing business which kept him very busy.

"Lynn will stay with us during her pregnancy," her
mother said. "We haven't decided for sure, but we think
we'll probably place the baby for adoption."

She excused herself to answer the telephone and I
glanced at petite, pretty, 15 year old Lynn. Her eyes
were filling with tears. It appeared that "we" weren't
sold on the idea of relinquishing the coming baby.

So often a teenager hides the fact of her pregnancy
from her family -- even from herself, it seems. But Lynn
was different. Just a few weeks earlier she had been hos-
pitalized because of a bronchial condition. Her doctor
came into her room for a final check before releasing her

to go home. But he had an amazing announcement. She was
five weeks pregnant'

Lynn discussed her predicament:

An hour later Ron -- the baby's father -- came
in and I told him. He said we could cope with it.
Soon my mother arrived, and we told her together.
She was, of course, upset, and most of all, hurt.
She went home and told my Dad. I was discharged
from the hospital late that afternoon.

And would you believe that all three of my
out-of-state sisters called me that night -- for
no special reason -- and we told them. My
grandmother also called. It was weird how fast
they all knew about it that same night.

There were so many options open because I was
only five weeks pregnant. Abortion would be the
first thing to think about if you didn't want a
baby. But I couldn't do that. We talked and
talked. Ron came over on Sunday and we talked
with my parents for a long time. We finally decided I would live at home during the pregnancy.
Then if we still loved each other, we would get
married after the baby was born.

Lynn continued going to school each day, but a few
weeks later she made the phone call to the special class for
pregnant students. She enrolled in the class the Monday
following our visit.

By chance she sat at Jodie's table. Jodie was the only girl in the class considering adoption. Her baby was due
in a couple of weeks, and she had only recently decided relinquishing was the best choice for her baby and for herself.
She and Lynn talked, but there wasn't time for much. Jodie
delivered her little boy two weeks later and returned to her
former school. She came back to the class only for a brief
visit.

A few days before Christmas vacation I brought up
the subject of adoption. Once more the tears started, and I
realized the time wasn't right. *"We* haven't decided," was

all she said.

A couple of months later Lynn told me her decision. She had decided to let her sister, who lives several hundred miles away, care for the baby "until I grow up." The decision was the result of a phone call her mother had made to her grandmother. She mentioned that Lynn might place the baby for adoption. This was related to the married sister who then called her mother. She urged them to let her have the baby.

"Before the baby goes out of the family, I want to care for it. Don't place it with strangers," she pleaded.

By this time Lynn had decided to see no more of Ron. As she describes him, "He thinks he's the big man. He drinks a little booze, then decides he can rule the world. He even dated someone else, and I thought if I couldn't depend on him now when I needed him the most, how could I ever depend on him?"

Lynn seemed satisfied with the decision to place the baby with her sister for the time being. She was a tenth grader, but realized she could skip a year, earning her high school diploma just a year later. She planned then to move in with her sister and her baby, and attend the nearby university.

Lynn's baby was born. Her mother coached her during labor and delivery, and the three of them came back to class a few days later to share the experience. Then, a week after his birth, Brad went home with Diana, Lynn's sister. Lynn remembers:

> The hardest thing I have ever done in my entire life was to hand Brad to Diana as she got on that airplane. I had cared for him a week, and it was rough sending him away. I don't think I could have done it if I hadn't known I would soon see him again.
>
> I went to see him about a month later. It was terribly hard leaving him again. But each time I visited him, and I did at least once a month that first year, it got a little easier.

As time passed, I realized I simply wasn't ready to take care of a baby. And I didn't want to pawn him off on my Mom and Dad.

So I finally came to my senses and decided the only way I could cope with it and be the person I wanted to be was to let my sister adopt him. So I signed the papers when he was almost two years old, and I haven't regretted one bit of it. I see him every once in a while, and he's doing just fine.

Now almost 18, Lynn has her own apartment and a job she enjoys. When asked if she felt she had missed something by skipping that year of high school, she replied:

No way. In fact, I can't imagine myself in high school this year. Maybe it would be fun going back, but I love where I am now. College maybe. I think I'll take a class or two this summer, and perhaps get into college this fall.

When Brad was born, though, no one could have told me I would adopt that baby out. I would never have believed them. And I don't regret that I didn't do it sooner. If I had when he was born, I don't know how I would have felt. But in that 1½ years I realized there was no way I could take care of him in the way I wanted him taken care of. By then he was already walking and saying a few words.

It was a hard decision. If I had thought Brad would have been better off with me, I would have taken him. But no way. He is in the best home I can imagine. He is so loved in that family. I couldn't see ruining a good thing.

So many people say they have never seen a family adoption work, but he's two years old and there simply is no problem.

I guess it's a lot because of the way I feel. I feel when I'm ready to have my family, I'll start it. I don't want to have my family too early when I can't deal with it.

"Did the girls in the class influence you?"

No, I don't think so. It did bother me when they said, "How could you do that?" I thought to myself, "How could they do that to their babies?" I didn't mean it in spite. It just seemed too hard, not only for them, but for their babies. I think I'm a lot happier person now without having a child, and I think Brad is happier where he is. I don't see how girls who are 14, 15, even 16, can have a baby, perhaps get married. . .how can they deal with it? I think if I had gone that route, I would be divorced now and would have had a sad life these past two years.

Lynn still sees Brad fairly often. Mike, the man she will marry in a few months, took her up to see him a few months ago, and Brad and his family spent Thanksgiving with Lynn and her parents.

When I go up there he feels just like another nephew. It isn't that I don't love him. . . I would do anything for him today. But I don't feel like I'm a mother now. . .and I'm not. I really never was except for that one week.

Perhaps I shouldn't say this because it may make me sound uncaring, but it wasn't hard for me to sign those adoption papers. Not nearly as hard as putting him on that plane when he was one week old. Of course it wasn't an easy breezy thing. . .I was nervous, but it wasn't terribly difficult because I had made my decision a month or two before. I didn't tell anybody for a while because I wanted to make sure. I really thought through whether or not I would regret doing this, and I decided I would not. It would have been much harder to sign those papers when he was first born. I'm happy my sister was willing to take him then without the final adoption decision.

Soon after I learned I was pregnant and was still attending my old school, I worked for a teacher in the activities office. She and I were alone one day, talking. I had told her I was pregnant, and she brought me a little newspaper clipping. I think that little article influenced me as much as anything. I think I still have it. . .Yes, here it is. . .

Dear Abby,

I am 16 and eight months pregnant. I made an important decision a few weeks ago. I decided to give my baby up for adoption. Abby, I love this baby very, very much. That is why I'm giving it up. Some people say I am cruel and even selfish, but I think it would be much more selfish to keep the baby and make it suffer for my mistakes.

I have always respected your opinion, Abby. Do you think I made the right choice?

Expecting the Best in Texas

Dear Expecting. Yes. God bless you.

I think this had a big effect on me. You have got to consider what is best for your baby. It's not like playing house. It's not like dressing him up and showing him off -- it's the real thing. You have got to realize your baby has to have the best. It's not only you that matters.

When I was pregnant, I thought, "How can I do this, how can I adopt my baby out?" But it was the best thing for the baby and I feel now it was the best for me.

VERA'S SITUATION

Vera never considered adoption while she was pregnant. She "knew" she would keep her baby and raise it herself. While she was pleasant to the two girls who were relinquishing that semester, she had commented to me, "How could anyone give up her baby?"

But she discovered that caring for a baby full time was harder than she had expected. She began to wonder, much as she loved Grant, if perhaps the baby would be better off with someone more ready to settle down to the constant care he demanded:

I never thought I would let anybody else take care of him, but it happened. I wasn't able to give him all the things he needed, and besides, I really didn't know how to take care of him.

Grant's father and I met when I was 14. We were going to get married as soon as I turned 16. But the first time I saw him hold Grant, I thought, "He can't do that." I couldn't realize the baby was his too. From that minute I knew we would break up. So one day I said, "You know, I'm not going to marry you," and he left.

Being pregnant was so neat. I remember when he would kick me and the funny feelings I'd get in my stomach -- it felt like butterflies. And sometimes when I was lying on the couch, he would turn completely around. Once a friend brought a stethoscope over, and I could feel his heart beat. It was weird.

But after he was born it was hard getting up in the middle of the night every single night. Every time he cried I picked him up, and I had trouble taking care of him without falling asleep myself. Then he'd wake up again early in the morning, and in the afternoon when I wanted to take a nap. God, I was tired!

You have to clean him, change his diapers, clean up his room so it won't smell, wash his clothes, mix his formula just right. But first you have to find the right one or he'll be sick. He had a lot of problems with formula. I took him to another doctor who said he was getting too much solid food. He put Grant on plain cereal and not much of that. He was about two months old then, and he started feeling better.

When he was six months old, I decided I couldn't handle it. I asked my sister-in-law to take him, but she wouldn't. She already had a baby two months younger than Grant.

So I tried a little longer. But if you go to school, you don't have time to take care of a baby. He was beginning to think my mother was his real mom. And I didn't think that was good. He'd be confused at having two moms.

Then we called my sister in Arizona. She already has two kids and she said she would be glad to take Grant. She hasn't adopted him -- she's just his legal guardian.

But Marge (my sister) couldn't come get him for almost a month, so my Mom took over. Sometimes people criticized me because I wasn't taking care of him myself. But I felt I was missing out on things with my friends and I didn't want that any longer. I feel kind of bad about that now -- I should have taken care of him until he left. Now I miss him and want to go see him.

What hurt me the most was the day he left. He had just learned to crawl and I wanted to sit and watch him crawl forever!

"You talked to an adoption agency counselor, didn't you?"

Yes, once. But I couldn't stand the thought of never seeing Grant again. I feel better knowing where he is and that I can keep in touch with him. When he's old enough to understand, I'll probably ask him if he would like to come back to live with me. But if he says no, I'll understand.

I want him to know I gave him to my sister because I love him, because I wanted him to have the things and the care he needed. I think I did the right thing. Some people don't understand, but I know why I did it. As long as I know, that's what counts.

"How do you think your sister would feel if you took him back?"

She'd be hurt, I know. She'd probably feel like I did when Grant left. When I heard that car drive away and I knew he was gone, I went in my bedroom and cried and cried. But I had to think -- what would I have done if I had kept him with no money? I couldn't have handled it.

"Any advice for other 14- or 15-year-olds?"

Talk it over with someone you don't even know, a total stranger. . .but make it clear you just want to know how somebody else feels. You'll have to make your own decision.

Then don't make that mistake again! Don't be fooled by anybody saying he loves you. At 14, 15, even 16 -- that's too young to understand motherhood, too young to take care of a baby. You still want your mother to take care of you at the same time you have to care for your baby.

There are too many things to do -- going to school, taking care of the baby, just too many things pushed at you if you get pregnant. You can't live out the rest of your childhood -- you have to be a woman already. You'll never have the experience of being a teenager. I wish I had thought first.

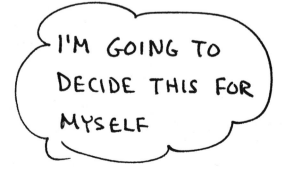

ADOPTIVE MOTHER EXPLAINS

Vince's mother also thought she could handle being a teenage parent. In fact, Vince was her second baby. But her life became harder and harder. Her babies' father never helped support his children and welfare didn't stretch far enough. Life was a drag. Vince's adoptive mother, Maria, tells his story:

Vince was 6½ months old when we took him. This was a sudden thing. Teresa is my husband's sister, and we knew she had a lot of problems. Then one day she called the family together because she didn't see how she could care for her kids any longer.

She had two, Elisa who was three, and Vince. Teresa was 18 then, and welfare was on her back. They kept threatening to take both children away from her. She knew by then she couldn't handle it, being a mother, but she wanted the kids to stay in the family.

So she said she wanted each of her brothers to take one. Elisa went with Jose up north and they adopted her. But that's been a problem because Teresa lives in the same town. She visits Jose's family often and brings presents just for Elisa. She ignores their other kids and that makes it hard for all of them.

We got away from that kind of pressure. We live about 200 miles away from the rest of them.

But when we went through legal adoption, it got complicated. First, Teresa called us several times and said she might change her mind. But then she said she really couldn't keep him. Later his father turned up and said flatly he wouldn't release him to us. So we had to go through court and prove abandonment. We could do this because he had never provided any support at all for Vince.

Once we got to court, there was no problem. It's official now. We still don't visit the family much because I think it's hard for Teresa. But they tell us she's getting her life back together now.

I thought at first we would just baby-sit for a while. I was pretty insecure about the whole thing until I heard that judge say, "This is your son." How we celebrated that night!

When we first got him, I got the after-baby blues which really surprised me. He cried a lot the first couple of days -- I guess we all did. Now, of course, I'm glad it happened. I had never understood before why anybody would give up their child. But now I have a great deal of respect for Teresa that she didn't fight for him when it came down to the line at court. I know it was hard for her. I know she decided to let us adopt him because she knew she couldn't take care of him and because she loved him.

She called us a month ago about a family matter. I called Vince and asked him if he wanted to speak to Teresa. He's three now, and of course he knows that we adopted him. "You remember Teresa, don't you?" I asked him.

He thought a minute, then said, "Oh, yes, she used to be my mommy, didn't she?" and he trotted off to talk to her on the phone.

I think it's worked out well for all of us.

MINORITY ADOPTION

Because family ties are especially strong in the Mexican American culture, adoption occurs less frequently than it does in Anglo and Black families. When it does occur, family adoption, as in Vince's case, is more apt to happen than is agency adoption. Someone in the extended family will often help the birth mother/father when parenting becomes too hard.

However, Los Angeles adoption agency social workers report a significant number of minority adoptions. A Chicano social worker commented that when he speaks to classes of pregnant teenagers, he passes his card out individually to the girls rather than to the teacher. "Sometimes they just want to talk," he commented, "and if there were less peer group or parental pressure they might choose to release for adoption."

At one time few adoptive homes were available in Black or Mexican American communities. However, this situation has changed. "We don't have healthy Black or Chicano babies waiting for placement," Janice Wills, Los Angeles County Department of Adoptions social worker, reported. "We have plenty of homes available for Chicano babies. In fact, we're now studying Chicano families who registered one and two years ago. There simply aren't enough babies free for adoption by those who wish to adopt."

Ms. Wills also stated that in the past it was assumed that middle class white girls placed their babies for adoption while Black teenagers always kept their infants. "I think this has changed," she said. "Now there is no big difference between whether the Black girl or the white girl keeps. This is certainly true with my clients."

More than one-third of the *children* (not necessarily infants) relinquished to public and private agencies in California in 1976 were Mexican American, Black, other nonwhite ethnic origin, or of mixed ethnic origin.

CRITICISM OF RELATIVE ADOPTION

A criticism often leveled at family adoption is that the child may be "claimed" by both his birth and adoptive parents. If the birth mother lives near or with her child, it can be frustrating and painful to see someone else bring up her son or daughter. She may disagree strongly with the way "her" child is being reared. If she does, should she interfere? Or should she ignore the situation, knowing the child is no longer truly hers?

Judging from the stories of relative adoption told in this chapter, the best approach is truly to release to that relative the *full* responsibility for the child. Sharing the parenting role, while difficult for the parents, can be especially damaging to the child. Every child needs the security of knowing *one* set of parents is truly his.

For many young parents, watching their baby reared by someone else may be too difficult. Releasing their child to strangers -- a couple carefully selected by their agency -- may be a better approach both for themselves and for their baby.

Agency – independent – relative – three kinds of adoption, and each is legal in most states. Each method has its good points and its not-so-good aspects. Only you can decide which, if any, is best for you and for your baby.

CHAPTER 6

Fathers Have Rights

What rights should fathers have? What rights *do* fathers have?

Married couples, of course, normally share parental rights. If a married woman wishes to release her baby for adoption, her husband must also sign the legal relinquishment -- even if he is not the child's father.

Until a few years ago, however, an unmarried father's permission was not required if the mother wished to give the baby up for adoption. Only the mother's signature was needed. A few states also require her parents' signatures if she is a minor.

A 1972 U.S. Supreme Court ruling, Stanley vs. Illinois, has had a great impact on the legal aspects of adoption. And this case didn't even involve an adoption!

When Stanley's common-law wife died, the court attempted to take his children away from him because he had not been married to their mother. The case went to the Supreme Court which ruled that the unwed father had a right to a legal hearing before his biological children could be taken away from him. He must at least be notified fully of a hearing on the termination of his parental rights.

Not all states have interpreted this ruling in the same way. Just how involved unmarried fathers should be in adoption proceedings hasn't been cleared by the courts.

States Vary in Interpretation

Courts and agencies in some states insist that both parents must consent to the release of a child. In other states, the father, if he is known, must simply be notified that the birth mother is relinquishing their child for adoption. If the father can't be found, agencies usually try to locate him. If they are unsuccessful after a certain period of time, the child can then be released for adoption.

"Current" legislation is tabulated by state in *Adoptions Without Agencies* by Meezan, Katz, and Russo (1). At the time it was published (1978), sixteen states did not provide through legislation for the consent of the father to the adoption of his illegitimate child (p. 150). Twenty-three states had passed legislation requiring the unmarried father's consent to his child's adoption "if the father has established or acknowledged paternity, or the child has been legitimated" (p. 152).

Iowa has a unique law which states, "Parental rights must be terminated in all instances (of adoption); appointed guardian must consent" (p. 163). The remaining ten states, California, Delaware, Illinois, Michigan, Montana, Rhode Island, Utah, Virginia, Washington, and Wisconsin, have passed laws putting the unmarried father in about the same position with regard to consent requirement as is the unmarried mother (p. 152). Even among these states, however, variations exist.

The authors state (p. 152): "It is evident that the unwed father's consent is required only in certain somewhat limited circumstances. In the vast majority of the states the burden is placed upon the father to assert his paternal interest in his child before his parental rights in that child will be guaranteed by the state. A balance is thus struck between the necessity of giving the unmarried

---

1. Meezan, William, Sanford Katz and Eva Manoff Russo. *Adoptions Without Agencies: A Study of Independent Adoptions.* 1978. New York: Child Welfare League of America, Inc.

father an opportunity to be a parent to his child and the need to facilitate placement of the child."

CALIFORNIA LAW

The Uniform Parentage Act is a California law which became effective in 1976. A major aim of this Act is to erase the former distinction in status between legitimate and illegitimate children. This was accomplished, but the Act presents a confusing situation to those dealing with adoption of children whose parents are not married to each other.

Does the unmarried father, for instance, have a right to insist his baby's mother must raise that baby herself (without his help) even if she feels adoption is the best decision?

Stacey, after a great deal of painful soul searching, finally decided adoption was the best option for her baby. She had another year of high school, and she had always wanted to be a teacher. She knew she wanted to go to college and, although she wanted a family some day, this wasn't the right time.

But what about Curt? He, of course, also had to sign to relinquish the baby. He and Stacey weren't seeing each other, but Pat, the adoption agency social worker, pointed out that he had to be involved too. In the meantime, Curt had been discussing his situation with a young minister. He decided to bring him along for the conference with Stacey and Pat.

They met, first together, then Curt and Pat talked while Stacey and the young pastor discussed the situation. He told Stacey he didn't think Curt should keep the baby nor should he marry Stacey because he was too immature for either marriage or parenthood.

However, the minister admonished Stacey, *she* must not relinquish -- she must keep the baby

"because in the Bible no unmarried mother gives
her baby up for adoption"!

Later that day Stacey discussed the situation with *her* pastor. He reminded her of Moses.
"Now there was an adoptee who *really* made good,"
he commented wryly.

Curt finally agreed to sign relinquishment
papers. The adoption proceeded smoothly from
that point only because he did so.

Two "Kinds" of Fathers

The California Uniform Parentage law describes two
kinds of fathers, "presumed" and "alleged." A man who
has lived with the mother, is married to her when the child
is born, or was married to her 300 days or less before
the birth is usually considered the "presumed" father. If
the mother doesn't wish to keep the child, he has the right
to custody. Before that child can be placed for adoption,
both parents must sign relinquishment -- or court action
must terminate parental rights.

Of course a joint relinquishment decision is pref-
erable for all those concerned with the adoption:

When Ronda decided she couldn't give her
baby the kind of life she wanted for him, she
told her former boy friend. Both of them discussed the situation with Pat.

Dennis seriously considered keeping the
baby. Ronda, though she would have preferred
not to know where her baby was, didn't oppose
Dennis' plans. She knew she wasn't ready to
care for the baby, but if Dennis' mother wanted
to help him, more power to them. She had always thought very highly of Mrs. Aguerre.

Dennis and the social worker discussed the
pros and cons of keeping vs. relinquishing.

Dennis decided that even though his mother
was willing to do so, she shouldn't quit her

job because of his child. Since he was still in
school, he knew he would have to have her help
if he became an "acting" father.

So Dennis and Ronda decided together to relinquish. Each seems satisfied with the decision.

Ronda and Dennis, although never married, had lived
together briefly early in her pregnancy. A "presumed" father (or fathers!) may be established, however, even if the
person(s) in question have neither lived with nor been married to the mother. California Civil Code 7004 (a) (4) states
a man may be presumed to be the father if "he receives the
child into his home and openly holds out the child as his natural child."

In addition, a man who doesn't meet these liberal requirements as the presumed father may, nevertheless, be
considered the "alleged" father. This happens if he is named
as the father but does not meet the above requirements. The

law still protects his rights in California by requiring his relinquishment, waiver of notice, or denial of paternity before a child relinquished by its unmarried mother can be placed.

In other words, the mother may name the father, and he may meet none of the above "presumed" father requirements. If she does, her child cannot be released for adoption until the man named either denies he is the father, waives (gives up) in writing his rights to notice of the adoption hearing, or signs relinquishment for adoption.

The father who does not make a decision creates a difficult situation for the mother:

Mario had said he might sign a paper denying he was the baby's father *or* he might sign for the relinquishment. He hadn't decided which he would do when the baby was born.

After his son's birth, he went to the hospital. First he stopped to see Sue. He said he wanted to see the baby. Sue, however, told him he couldn't see the infant unless he signed the relinquishment papers as the child's father.

She knew he was the father. He knew it. He was listed on the birth certificate as the baby's father. If he chose to say at that point he was not, she was resigned to it. But she was firm in saying he had no right to see the baby unless he admitted paternity. And she was correct. He had no legal right to see a baby against its mother's wishes unless he admitted to being the baby's father.

He decided to admit paternity *and* sign relinquishment papers. As soon as he signed, he went to the nursery where he took several pictures of his son.

―――――――

If the mother reports that she doesn't know who the father is or if the alleged father cannot be located, court action is still necessary to terminate his parental rights.

"The baby has two parents. The rights of both parents have to be terminated before the child is free for adoption," explained Janice Wills, Los Angeles County Department of Adoptions social worker. "A presumed father has legal rights; an alleged natural father's rights are determined by the court unless he waives his rights for that determination. That court action is called '7017.'

"Sometimes the father's whereabouts are unknown to the girl," Ms. Wills continued, "but every effort is made to locate him. We use whatever information the young woman can remember. His last known address? Any relatives? Friends? Neighbors? Occupants on either side of his last address? We also request information from the Department of Motor Vehicles. We check DMV records not only in California but also in any other state where the baby's mother thinks the father has or might have lived as an adult.

"If the alleged father is not located, the court grants the 7017 based on the agency's proof of complete search and the girl's detailed statement concerning their relationship.

"Some girls are telling us they don't know who the father is," she commented. "If the natural mother denies knowledge of who the father is, gives us no name, we still have to do a 7017 court action against him as an unknown father. Sometimes we believe she does know who the baby's father is even if she denies it. In such cases, we hold the social worker responsible for using a lot of care.

"When this happens to me -- the girl tells me she has no idea who the father is -- I try to explain why it is important that we notify him of her plans. We don't want a man coming back later and saying, 'I heard _____ had a baby and we lived together for a while. If I had known she had that baby, I would have supported it. *I intend to do everything I can to get my baby.*'

"If she gives a baby up for adoption, she wants to be sure no one can come back later and make an unhappy situation," Ms. Wills concluded.

David Leavitt, the Beverly Hills, California, attorney

who specializes in independent adoptions, is backing pro-
posed state legislation concerning the rights of the alleged
father. Under this legislation, if passed, the man named
as father of the child could simply be notified that he is alleged to be -- could be -- the father of this child. After
such notification, he would have to file within 30 days to
establish the father-child relationship. If he didn't do
so, the child could be released without his signature.

FATHER CAN STOP ADOPTION

The California law is an attempt to protect the
rights of both birth parents. But Charlotte De Armond,
Children's Home Society of California, reports some girls
who would prefer to relinquish for adoption are keeping
their babies because if they don't, the father says he will.
And sometimes the young mother knows this would not be
in the best interests of her baby. Yvette felt this way:

When Yvette told her parents she was pregnant, there was a terrible scene. In fact, her
mother demanded she get an abortion. Yvette
talked to David, her 17 year old boy friend.
They decided to go to San Francisco where they
could live with David's brother and his family.

For two or three weeks Yvette enjoyed the
change. But there wasn't enough money, the
house was a mess, and David's two little neph-
ews drove her crazy. So she decided to go home.

Yvette and her mother somehow overcame their
differences and became closer than they had ever
been. Both her mother and father suggested
adoption, but Yvette was adamant. This was her
baby and, David or no David, she would raise it.

About a month before her due date, however,
Yvette changed her mind. She wanted to play
softball this summer -- a small thing, perhaps.
But if, because of her baby, she couldn't play
ball whenever she wanted, what else would she
miss during her teen years? She wanted to enjoy her two remaining years of high school, be

able to participate in school activities as she
had always done. Maybe motherhood should be post-
poned after all. She talked to an adoption agency
social worker several times. Her mind was made
up. She would give up her baby.

The social worker got in touch with David. He
had come back to live with his mother, but he and
Yvette weren't seeing each other. In fact, Yvette
had become thoroughly disenchanted with his lack
of interest in school, his current involvement in
drugs. She knew their relationship was over.

For two weeks after his first appointment with
the social worker, David threatened to keep the
baby himself. His mother would help him raise it.
But after several discussions with Yvette, he said
he would sign for relinquishment as soon as the
baby was born.

Three weeks later Yvette delivered a seven
pound girl. After a hospital visit from David and
his mother, Yvette put in a panic call to her social worker.

"He says if I give the baby up he'll take it
to court and get custody," wailed Yvette. "The
last thing I want is for him and his mother to
raise this baby. You know what kind of home they
have -- she's on welfare and doesn't even take
good care of the kids she has. And imagine David
taking care of a baby! Can we stop them?"

The social worker consulted her supervisor.
Regretfully she told Yvette and her family that
they couldn't guarantee the outcome of such a
court case. "It's as if we're on shifting sand,"
she explained. "So much depends on the judge.
Two years ago we could assure a mother that if she
had already signed a relinquishment, she could
rescind (take it back) if the baby's father won
custody. She could still raise the baby herself
if she thought the father would be a poor parent.

"Now, however," she said, "we simply don't

know how the judge will decide. The fact that
you lived with David that month in San Francisco
undoubtedly makes him the 'presumed' father in
the eyes of the court. And the presumed father
has the same rights as the mother."

Yvette decided not to take the risk. She is
raising her baby herself.

Stacey, whose baby's father insisted she "should"
raise the baby herself, resented the struggle she had to go
through during pregnancy. It was hard enough making the
decision to release her baby for adoption. Having to con-
front Curt and his pastor and defend that decision was extremely frustrating.

However, when she was asked her opinion of the
law concerning fathers' rights, she said thoughtfully:

I feel it is necessary. The father has the
right and he should sign the relinquishment papers. It makes it harder for the mother sometimes -- I should know! -- but you can't just
forget about his rights.

If you have decided to or are thinking about releasing your baby for adoption, check the law in your own
state. If you are married, of course both you and your
husband must sign the papers. A significant number of
married couples voluntarily release children for adoption each year, according to adoption statistics.

If you are single, carefully check with an adoption
agency the laws concerning fathers' rights in your area.
It is important to you -- and to your baby -- that the adoption occur as smoothly as possible.

And it is *extremely* important that *all* legal aspects are handled properly.

CHAPTER 7

Dealing with Grief

Is it easy to surrender a baby for adoption? *Of course not!*

Giving a baby up for adoption causes some of the same emotions a mother feels if she loses her baby through death. She will (or should) go through the same kind of grieving process. If she doesn't, if she simply pushes her grief out of her mind and "forgets the whole thing," she may have emotional problems later.

A young woman in Oregon, who hadn't allowed herself to grieve when her baby was placed, described her need to mourn later:

Twelve years ago I put my baby up for adoption. I was 17 when I became pregnant. Everything was very hush-hush back then. I grew up in a strongly religious home, and my pregnancy was a disgrace. We didn't want the neighbors to know, so I went back to Missouri to live. A doctor and his family took me in.

About the only good thing that happened to me that year was that beautiful family. They gave me lots of love and acceptance that I hadn't had as I was growing up.

I chose to relinquish because I knew that was the only thing I could do. I always knew my

decision was right. . .my problem was that I
didn't grieve. I just stuffed it all down inside me.

I know nothing about my child excepting its
sex and weight. I was in a labor room by myself across from the nursery. I was heavily se-
dated during labor and delivery. After the baby was born, they took it away immediately.
Then I saw the blinds shut down in the nursery
and I heard a baby cry. I'll never forget that
cry!

As soon as I was able, I returned to Oregon
and finished school. I got a job, was married
a couple of years later. We have two children
now.

But last year I began to realize I had some
serious problems -- I felt depressed and wasn't
handling it well at all. So I went to see my
pastor for counseling.

Lots of feelings have come out in these
counseling sessions. This year I've been going
through the stages of grief that I simply
skipped twelve years ago! It was very difficult for me. Sometimes I would call my counselor and say, "Why am I crying?" He would
suggest that I might be having a delayed reaction. We would talk about what was happening
and try to deal with it.

If you are releasing a child, you need to
know what the grieving process is. You will
have to go through it. You should realize what
the stages of grief are. . .to realize it's OK
to deny your grief, to be angry, to be depressed, to feel rejected. And finally, if you
go through these stages and you don't try to
bury your grief, you will feel acceptance. It's
OK to have these feelings. That's been so important to me, to work through these feelings
no matter how long it takes.

Patricia Schwiebert, R.N., Educational Coordinator for the University of Oregon Health Sciences Center, pointed out, "Of course a mother who gives up her baby grieves. And sometimes we put road blocks in her way. We say, 'Well, it wouldn't have worked out anyhow. You're too young to be a mother. You'll feel better soon.' All of this may be true, but that isn't what she needs to hear now. She knows it is *better* or she wouldn't have made this decision, but she is grieving nevertheless.

"She has already bonded with her baby before birth. Right now she is grieving because she lost her child. You support her feelings at this point. Sometimes we have gotten girls who are relinquishing in touch with others who did so in the past. They can share how they feel."

SEEING BABY BEFORE ADOPTION

At the Salvation Army White Shield Home in Portland, Oregon, some young mothers have chosen rooming-in with their babies in the hospital even though they have decided to release for adoption. Several have breastfed their babies during those few days in the hospital. They give numerous reasons for doing so, such as "wanting my baby to know me," "wanting my baby to have the benefits of colostrum," and "wanting my baby to know love immediately from birth," according to Sen Speroff, nurse-midwife.

"Babies at our hospital who are being released for adoption still are usually marked 'DNS' (Do Not Show), but if the mother chooses rooming-in and breastfeeding, obviously that rule is not followed!" commented Ms. Speroff.

She spoke strongly about the rights of the pregnant woman who is relinquishing her baby for adoption. "Because you are releasing doesn't mean you get a glimpse of your baby once in the nursery and that's it," Ms. Speroff pointed out. "Your right as an adopting mother is that you may see your baby as much as you want, you may care for your baby. If you start wavering in the hospital, you have the option of foster care for a short time while you make up your mind. If you decide to keep your baby, you need to remember that adoption is still available two days from now . . .or a year from now."

In this Portland hospital, quite a few mothers have coached their teenage daughters during labor. "I feel the parents' presence during the prenatal period and through labor is important," commented Ms. Speroff, "because the girl is going through the death of a relationship, the adoption. And the grandparents are also going through a grieving period. This is their grandchild, their flesh and blood. And we need to support them too.

"Sometimes the parent and daughter need to cry together. If her family is not included, they may say, 'OK, it's been a month, why are you still moping around the house? You should get on with your life.' But we don't get over the death of a sister in a month. Why would you forget about a baby in a month? If the grandparents have been involved, they may understand what she is going through. Maybe that sharing will bring this family closer together," she added.

Jodie mentioned that she hadn't grieved a great deal. Unexpectedly, she took her baby home for two days because she couldn't reach her adoption worker on

Christmas Day. She hadn't planned even to see her son:

> I didn't really grieve excepting for the first
> couple of days. I was fine until I had to start
> getting his things ready for the adoption worker.
> It was time to feed him and I couldn't make my-
> self do it. So my sister took over, and I know
> it was hard on her too. She said, "We'll just
> think of him as if he is dead."
>
> "I will not think of him that way," I said.
> "He is not dead, and we won't write him off as
> if he were."
>
> I knew that he would be better off where he
> was going. I had placed him in God's hands, and
> I knew He couldn't fail me. It was through my
> faith that I did it. I don't believe I would
> have made it on my own.

Caring for her baby those two days was undoubtedly
an emotionally healthy situation for Jodie, hard as it was
for her. This gave her "closure" in the act of adoption.
It made her baby very real to her, and her grieving, while
short-lived, was intense.

Janice Wills, a Los Angeles social worker, agreed
that seeing the baby before it is released for adoption is
wise. She thinks it completes the adoption in a positive
way. "The baby is not a stranger," she commented. "She
has carried that baby all this time.

"Sometimes a girl will say that if she sees her baby,
she won't be able to give it up. This hasn't happened in my
experience. I think seeing the baby reinforces whatever
decision she has already made." Ms. Wills suggests that
seeing the baby through the nursery window may be enough
for some girls, that feeding the baby for several days can
make it extremely hard to give him up.

FATHERS GRIEVE TOO

Often the baby's father needs to grieve too. I realized this when I visited Ellen who had relinquished her
baby a year earlier. To my surprise, her baby's father

was there when I arrived. I hadn't known they were seeing
each other again.

Carl appeared upset as Ellen talked. He
played nervously with the bracelets she had tak-
en from her arm. He looked alert, smiled at the
right places as she told her story. But occasionally he appeared close to tears.

Ellen's mother had explained quietly that
Carl was back in the picture, that to her amazement she and Ellen's father thought the world of
him. When Ellen was pregnant, her baby's father
was almost never mentioned. Her mother had told
me Ellen didn't know his name. As I guessed at
the time, I soon learned this wasn't so. But he
and Ellen didn't see each other during her pregnancy, and I assumed he was gone.

Ellen's lawyer had somehow gotten Carl's
signature for waiver of his rights in the adoption proceeding. At the time, because of parental pressure, Ellen would have nothing to do
with him. His parents had moved across town,
and he had enrolled in another high school. He
was 16, a tenth grader, and he was trying to
forget the whole mess.

When the lawyer called, he was scared. He
was told rapidly of his rights, with the added
comment that the waiver would be the "simplest"
unless, of course, he wanted to deny paternity.
So he signed the waiver.

A year later he saw Ellen again. They started dating, and had become close again. As I
talked with Ellen, she urged me to include him
in the interview. I hesitated, not wanting to
pry, not wanting to hurt him. But we started
talking.

While Ellen was sure she had made the right
decision in releasing the baby for adoption,
Carl obviously was not so sure. He seemed depressed, burdened with guilt fee ings. As he

talked, it became evident he hadn't shared his feelings about the adoption with anyone. Ellen was so sure of the rightness of the adoption -- how could he burden her with his feelings of loss?

"Just talking about this today is impressive," he said. "Somehow I feel better."

Fathers often experience *denial* of grief more intensely and for a longer period of time than do the mothers. This may give others (and themselves) the impression that they aren't experiencing any effects from the loss of the baby.

Apparently Carl had not allowed himself to grieve while the adoption was taking place. Only now, many months later, was he facing his loss and dealing with it.

Often the father, as in Carl's situation, is simply behind time in his grieving. He may not experience the reality of the child until birth occurs. To the mother, the child was real throughout pregnancy, and her feelings of parenthood become even more intense at birth. If her child is released for adoption, she will grieve. The father may not . . .until later.

You Can Decide

In years past, a birth mother who was relinquishing often didn't see her baby. It was released for adoption, and she was supposed to forget the whole thing.

Today, most people working with birth parents who relinquish recommend that the mother see her baby before she releases. They feel it is healthier emotionally for her to do so. Sometimes they suggest holding him, perhaps even feeding him while they are in the hospital.

If you plan to surrender your baby, you may find, however, that someone -- perhaps a friend, a nurse in the hospital, possibly even your doctor -- tells you *not* to go near the baby, not to see him.

Be sure you make your own decision on this issue, too.

You may feel like Debbie (see next chapter), and be convinced it is better not to see your child. That's OK. But if you're not sure, you'll probably be better off looking at her, perhaps holding her.

If you see her, if she is "real" to you, this can help put a "closure" on your relinquishment. It can help you realize you are truly giving her up.

But if *you* know you don't want, couldn't bear to see and hold your baby, explain your thinking to the hospital personnel. You have a right to decide for yourself.

Above all, face the grief you'll surely feel. Don't hide it in the back of your mind and refuse to deal with it.

When and if you decide to give your baby up, you may find you go through the pain of "deciding" more than once. While you're pregnant, perhaps you'll "know" it's the best thing to do. After you deliver, you'll wonder if you're doing the right thing. And when you sign the final papers, you'll hurt again.

You may wonder as you face the final signing of relinquishment papers, "Why do I still hurt so much? If this is the right decision, should it *hurt?*"

Of course you'll hurt! You're losing a baby. But the hurt will gradually go away -- as long as you face your grief and don't try to bury it.

The best "therapy" while in this situation -- you're hurting and you wonder if it will ever stop -- is to talk with another birth mother who relinquished. Perhaps someone who gave her baby up several years ago will share with you how she feels now about her decision. Not that you will ever feel exactly like someone else -- but it often helps to share experiences.

You may also find it helps to write your child a letter telling her how much you love her and that it's precisely for that reason you're letting someone else love and care for her.

Or you may prefer to follow Debbie's example (next chapter) and write to your baby's adoptive family. Whether or not you meet them, your letter could mean a lot to them and to your/their child.

Final signing for relinquishment can be soon after you leave the hospital if you are releasing to an agency. Or it may be two months after your baby has been independently placed in an adoptive home. (Remember, the public agency in most states will do a home study after the baby is placed in independent adoption.)

Whenever you're hurting, perhaps especially at the final signing, you may think, "This is my baby, it's part of me." A poem by Kahlil Gibran may help:

> *And a woman who held a babe against*
> *her bosom said, Speak to us of Children.*
> *And he said:*
> *Your children are not your children.*
> *They are the sons and daughters of Life's*
> *longing for itself.*
> *They come through you but not from*
> *you,*
> *And though they are with you yet they*
> *belong not to you.*
>
> *You may give them your love but not*
> *your thoughts,*
> *For they have their own thoughts.*
> *You may house their bodies but not*
> *their souls,*
> *For their souls dwell in the house of to-*
> *morrow, which you cannot visit, not even*
> *in your dreams.*
> *You may strive to be like them, but seek*
> *not to make them like you.*

*For life goes not backward nor tarries
with yesterday.*

*You are the bows from which your chil-
dren as living arrows are sent forth.*
*The archer sees the mark upon the path
of the infinite, and He bends you with His
might that His arrows may go swift and far.*
*Let your bending in the archer's hand
be for gladness;*
*For even as He loves the arrow that flies,
so He loves also the bow that is stable.*

(*The Prophet* by Kahlil Gibran. 1963: Alfred A.
Knopf, Inc., p. 17-18.)

As Gibran says, our children are not ours, they go
through us. This thought applies not only to all parents
generally, but perhaps especially to birth parents who are
giving up their child to someone else when s/he is very
young.

CHAPTER 8

Birth Mothers Write Letters

Some birth mothers who release for adoption find that writing a letter to the baby helps them deal with their grief. Usually this letter is put into the agency file for the child to receive later. If the birth mother requests it, however, it generally can be given to the adoptive parents.

Other birth mothers prefer to write to the baby's adoptive parents. If the adoption is "closed," the letter, whether to the baby or to the parents, must contain no identifying information. (A "closed" adoption is one in which the birth mother and adoptive parents do not meet each other.)

Kirsten, who released her baby for adoption independently, said:

> I wrote a letter to the baby, about three pages. I wrote it while I was still pregnant. I also made some booties and a couple of blankets for him. We put it all in a package with the letter. The parents picked it up when they took him home from the hospital. Somehow that helped me, just thinking that he had something from me.

Suzanne, Tod's mother, had worried that when he grew up, her son might think she didn't love him because she gave him up. So she wrote him a long letter in which she explained why she had decided to release him to a family related to a friend of hers:

Dear Tod,

I don't exactly know where to start. I'm
going to try to explain to you why I gave you up
for adoption. I don't want you to think that it
was something I did out of resentment toward you
or not wanting you. I did want you. But then I
got to thinking that I was just being selfish.
I gave you up for adoption because I loved you,
and because I didn't feel that I could provide
the things that I wanted you to have.

I want you to have all the love that two
parents could give you. I wouldn't have been
able to do that. You see, your natural father
and I are not together, and I think it's best
that you have a father.

Besides that, I was too young and wasn't
ready to settle down to be a mother, and that
wouldn't have been very fair to you.

When I first decided to relinquish, I was
going to go through a private adoption agency.
Then I thought that was a cold way to give a
child up for adoption. You see, you pick the
parents out of a set of papers that tell about
them, but you don't really get to know them. I
wanted to know right away what I was about to
get myself -- and you -- into. I mean, after
all, I was about to make a decision that would
affect your whole life.

I met your parents through one of your cou-
sins. She told me about your mother and father
not being able to have any kids of their own,
and how they have been trying to adopt a child
for more than ten years.

I thought it over for a long time, and
thought that anybody who has been wanting a
child for ten years would be able to give you
all the love you need.

I felt it was best that I met the parents,

for I think meeting them made it easier for me.
When I was still in the hospital I saw your parents, and saw how happy they were. It made me
happy. I knew for sure then that you were going
to get a lot of love, much much more than I could
give you myself.

I hope in the future, when you are old enough
to understand, and if you want to, I will be able to meet you. Right now, I must stay out of
your life, for your parents and your sake as well
as my own.

I also hope you won't feel any bitterness
toward me. I don't think you will, because you
have a mother and father that love you very much.
Your parents are terrific people. I know for sure
I made the right decision, and I don't think I
could have picked better parents.

I hope everything goes right for you and that
you have a very happy life.

I love you.

Recently Suzanne happened to be in a park at the same time Tod was there with his parents. After she saw him, Suzanne wrote:

It was the happiest feeling I have ever had to see Tod so joyful with two lovely parents who love and care for him. It also made me happy to see a couple who couldn't have children by birth with a child of their own.

I don't think I will ever regret my decision. I know I wouldn't have it any other way. Girls who are thinking of adoption need to talk to girls who have put their child up for adoption and to others who thought of doing so but decided against it. They need a lot of information about the adoption procedure and about the parents. They should know they can choose to meet the parents -- that helped me so much. I knew what I was getting into. But I know others who wouldn't want to be this open.

WRITING BABY'S ADOPTIVE PARENTS

Debbie, too, was able to choose the family that would receive her baby. She relinquished through a public agency which gave her descriptions of several couples. From these descriptions she picked the family she thought would give her child the life she wanted him to have.

Unlike Suzanne, Debbie decided it would be better not to see her baby and not to meet his family. She also chose not to write a letter to her son but, rather, to write to his adoptive parents. She explains her thinking in the following letter to them:

Hello --

For weeks I've been trying to think of a way to start this letter. And as you can see, I couldn't come up with anything but a hello. I hope that's enough.

Now I'll explain the reasons for this letter. I was told by several people that if I wished, I could leave the child a letter for him to read when he gets older. But I decided against it, as I have also decided against seeing him, keeping the original copy of the birth certificate, naming him, or leaving my name on a list for him to find me if he should ever want to.

Do I sound like I'm being cold? The reason I'm doing this is because I told myself when I decided to relinquish that I had to give up *totally*. And all those things I just mentioned are reminders. In my opinion, I still wouldn't be giving him up completely.

I want you to know I really do love him. That's the reason I decided relinquishment.

You two can give him so much more than I ever could at my age.

It took so long for me to make this decision. And for a while I was strongly against it. I just couldn't imagine carrying him for nine months and then giving him up. The hardest thing to face was when a voice inside me said, "You're being selfish, you're not even thinking of what's best for the baby."

So with the help of many others, I realized the best thing was to give him up. And with the strength that God gave me it really wasn't that bad.

Now I look back on my pregnancy and thank God that I had him as long as I did. And I want you to know if I had it to do all over again, I would change nothing. It was the hardest nine months I've ever been through but there was something so beautiful about it that made it all worthwhile.

How does it feel to know I have a child out there I'll never know? Well, I'll tell you, it feels great! How can I explain. . .

I know that I have given him the most important thing, his life. That in itself is a bless-
ing. What's more, I've accepted the fact that
he'll be better off without me.

I also feel I've given you two a gift which
is rare in itself and hard to come by. How
could anyone give you something more beautiful
than a child. . .I hope you feel the same way.

There are so many things I have to say and
I can't keep them straight in my mind.

I think of you three often and my prayers
are always with you.

I want you to know that I don't think of myself as the mother in the full sense of the word.
True, I did carry him for nine months and gave
birth to him, but it seems to me that the hardest part of parenting is from the time the child
is an infant until he reaches maturity. While
he is in the womb is probably the easiest time a
mother will ever know. Parenting is surely the
hardest job on the face of the earth, and it's

the one least taught. In my opinion, people take it too lightly. Maybe it's because they don't want to accept the fact that it's that important or that hard.

I think the second hardest thing is relinquishment. But then, whoever said anything in life would be easy?

Whenever I start feeling down and think about the baby, something clicks in my mind and tells me that just because we will never be together in this life doesn't mean we won't be together in the second life.

In fact, my hopes are that at one time we will all be together. Not just the baby and I, but you two also.

When I decided to pick the family, I had no idea what it would mean. When the time came, as I sat with forms in my hand, forms describing different couples, I suddenly realized this was a child's life I was choosing. Your interests matched ours the most. And that's why I chose you. I am hoping that he will do a lot of things that he would have done if he were with me.

I will tell you more about myself in case he ever asks you.

I love music. I love all kinds of music. And I play the piano. I am an outdoors person. I love the mountains and especially enjoy the beach. I like going on motorcycle rides. (His father loves them.) I love to be alone every once in a while. And I like writing occasionally. I like people (they fascinate me), and life in general. My favorite subjects are English and history.

I love my faith and pray that he will also. Since my pregnancy I've no doubt that there is a God. I'd have given up a long time ago if there weren't.

If there is anything I ask of you, it is that you assure him that I love him and I always will. He doesn't need to look for me for we will be together sometime and that will be better.

Please write back. I'd love and appreciate it.

ADOPTIVE PARENTS RESPOND

Debbie sent her letter to the adoption agency social worker who delivered it to the baby's adoptive parents. Debbie did not know their name, of course, and her letter had no identifying information in it.

Three weeks later Debbie had a visit from the social worker. She came by to hand her the answer to her letter:

To our son's natural Mother,

We received your letter, and like you, we have so much we would like to say. Like you, we really don't know where to start.

The most important thing, I guess, is to say "Thank you." Somehow that doesn't seem like enough. You have given us something that is so unique -- not only a chance to share our love, but someone to treasure.

We can't tell you how happy you have made us. Our lives have always been full of love for one another, but now we feel so fulfilled. We've always wanted children, always talked about having four. But when God didn't send us any of our own, we felt there was a reason. Because we wanted children to share with one another and to share our lives, we applied for adoption. If I had carried him myself, he could be no more a part of us or loved more.

You are in our thoughts every day. When we

put him to bed I always tell our son how special
he is and how lucky he is to have two mommies
who love him very much. I've done that from the
day we brought him home and always will. He
doesn't understand now, but someday he will.

He is a beautiful, bright child with huge
eyes. We promise you we'll give him the best we
can, love, guidance -- all it takes to make him
happy and healthy. He will always know of your
love for him.

We took him to his first Mass on Christmas
Day. After Mass we had him blessed and lit two
candles, one for our new son and one for you.
We placed them in front of the Infant Jesus and
prayed. We want you to know this -- because
when you relinquished him to us, in our hearts a
part of you came too. What I'm trying to say is
-- even though we won't meet in this life, you
are a part of us. When we do meet in the hereafter, you won't have to tell us who you are,
for I feel we'll know you just as he will.

You have given us a gift of love and life.
If we are lucky enough to open our home to other
children, he will always be special. He has opened and filled our hearts. He is so loved. He
is so very special. And so are you.

How hard it must have been for you to pick
parents for him. You said your interests and
ours were most alike. They are -- and yes, he
will probably do a lot of the things he would
have done with you. His Daddy is already waiting
for him to be old enough to go camping.

If he shows an interest in something, we will
try to steer him in that direction -- but he will
never be pushed. You said you liked people --
well, that he already has proven, for he loves
to study new faces, and he smiles so big.

I hope you will find peace in knowing you

have made a childless couple so very happy. What we want in our lifetime is only the best for him.

Whenever you do think of the three of us, please think of us with love in our hearts and smiles on our faces -- and all because of the special you. Until we meet in the hereafter, peace, prayers, and all our love.

CHAPTER 9

Releasing a Toddler for Adoption

WHO AM I?

By TanelLe Garrison, 15 Year OLd Mother

> *I'm not sure who I am.*
> *Maybe you can help me.*
> *Am I a lost little girl. . .*
> *Or a grown woman?*
> *Surely you can help me.*
>
> *Yes, maybe I'll find who I am. . .*
> *Maybe I won't.*
> *And if by chance I don't,*
> *Maybe you can help me.*
>
> *What will happen if I never find*
> *   who I am?*
> *Will I die. . .or will I live. . .*
> *Am I a lost little girl*
> *Or a grown woman?*
> *Maybe I will never know.*

Tanelle speaks for many school age mothers. If a girl becomes a mother before she finds who she is herself, she may start wondering, "Who am I? Am I 'just' a mother? How do I have a life of my own now?"

The young mother with these thoughts may be a very

"good" mother. Tanelle certainly is. So was Lorraine. She shared her story of her two years with Luke:

I didn't consider relinquishment before delivery because my boy friend didn't want me to. At first, it was a pretty good experience, being a mother. I Loved him, and I still do.

That spring was neat. I was really into motherhood. Summer was OK, although I missed going to the beach every day as I used to do. Then I started dating and got back into basketball. I was so pleased when I lettered last year.

But times got harder. I have a sister a year older than I am, and seeing her free to go out whenever she wanted was difficult to take. I started going out a lot, too, and I'd leave Luke with my Mom. But I started thinking, "I'm not even taking care of him."

Then it got still harder to cope with him. When he was about 8½ months old, I told my Mom I was thinking of giving him up. She was all broken up, so I didn't talk about it again for a long time. But the idea of releasing him for adoption kept going through my mind.

It was almost a year later that I brought up adoption again. I had talked with a girl friend who has a child Luke's age. She's married, but she could understand how I felt. She told me I should do it if that's what I wanted.

So I talked with my family. My sister's boy friend knew a couple who wanted to adopt a little boy. She couldn't have any kids because she had had a hysterectomy. Sam told me all about them, and then I met them. We sat and talked for a long time. Luke started spending weekends with them and he adapted beautifully.

About two months later I signed the adoption papers.

My mother still sees Luke. His adoptive

mother never had a father, and she had always said she would welcome Luke's birth grandparents.   I see them once in a while too.

Sometimes I cry when I'm down because I miss him.

I learned, though, that it's best to go by what you feel.   Don't let anybody talk you out of what you want to do. Don't listen to other people.

You have to live with yourself.   Just do what you feel is right for you and for your baby.

Life hasn't been easy for Lorraine. Losing a son who is almost two years old is probably a great deal harder than losing a baby. Sure, bonding occurs during pregnancy, and giving up a baby is difficult. But Lorraine and Luke shared a lot in the time they had together. It took a great deal of courage (and some desperation) for Lorraine to do what she knew was best for her and for Luke.

She called recently. She still enjoys school and will graduate in two months. She sees Luke occasionally. In fact, she had taken him shopping the day before she called.

CHILD'S AGE AT RELINQUISHMENT

Almost nine out of ten children (89.4 percent) released for adoption to public or private agencies in California in 1970 were less than one month old (State of California, 1978: "Characteristics of Relinquishment Adoptions in California 1970–1975). By 1976, the percentage of babies released within the first month after birth had dropped not only in number (from 5,922 in 1970 to 1,178 in 1975), but also in percentage of the total from 89.4 percent to only 42.2 percent.

According to Janice Wills, social worker for the Los Angeles County Department of Adoptions, her department placed more than 500 children in 1978. About one-third of these children were toddlers, another third were older children, and only one-third were infants.

An example of the heartbreak in later placement is the letter a social worker received from a young mother who had relinquished two toddlers. "Please have a happy life. I hope you'll know me some day," she wrote. The letter, addressed to her children, will go in their file. It will be there for them when they are grown.

Maria Vargas-Pyle, Children's Home Society counselor, commented, "We're seeing teen mothers who considered adoption before birth. Often because of family pressure, they decided to keep the baby. But now a year or two later some are coming back. Sometimes they really start thinking about the tremendous responsibility of raising a child after they leave home and are living by themselves. Sometimes a boy friend doesn't want an instant family."

MICHELE'S STORY

At first Michele enjoyed parenting. Caring for her infant daughter went smoothly for a while. A few months later, however, she found it hard to cope with the demands of constant motherhood:

Remember how furious I was with my family most of the time I was pregnant? I had had it up to here with my Mom and Dad, our church, everything. I didn't mean to get pregnant -- at least, I don't think I did. But in a way I probably wanted to show them I didn't have to be the person they wanted me to be.

I wanted to be such a good mother. I loved working in the Infant Center while I was pregnant, and that Parent Psychology class was my favorite.

The first two or three months after Sharon was born were great. She was such a good baby. Sure, I had to get up in the middle of the night at first, but I didn't really mind. All she seemed to need then was to eat and sleep.

But then things changed.

("Things" had indeed changed. About the time Sharon was three months old, Michele had gotten involved again with friends who were into drugs. She didn't seem to

care about herself any more -- she didn't eat much, got terribly thin. She started making comments about her own lack of worth, what a poor mother she was, etc. She lived with her mother part of the time, and moved in with her boy friend periodically.)

I began to think Sharon wasn't getting what she needed. I didn't want to take care of her physical needs, but I knew I had to. And emotionally I realized I didn't cut it.

Michele talked of the time she hit bottom and knew she had to do something about Sharon. Finally she called Pat from Children's Home Society. They talked a long time. She explained to Pat that motherhood somehow wasn't working for her. She was tired of responsibility. She was tired of the hard work. She missed her freedom to come and go as she wished.

Pat came back the next day. She described a young family who lived near the beach. They had learned a year earlier that they could never have a child born to them, and they wanted to adopt.

The mother had been working in an insurance agency. She had recently quit her job to stay home and get ready for

the adopted baby they hoped to have soon. The father had a
good job. Both enjoyed the beach and sailing in their small
boat. They wanted to share their lives with a child. Michele
continued her story:

> Pat let me read their file. It was scary,
> thinking of Sharon, and having the power to
> choose a new family for her. But when I looked
> at what I was giving her, and then at what they
> could offer, I knew I had to do it. I loved her
> too much to keep on the way we'd been going.

Michele had several more counseling sessions with
Pat. She decided to sign the relinquishment papers. She
wrote a long letter to Sharon and asked Pat to give it to her
daughter's new parents. Pat did so, and Michele received
a short, unsigned note a few weeks later:

> "Thank you for the greatest gift anyone could
> ever give us. Sharon already is adjusting to her
> new home, and we love her. We're already telling
> her about her first mother who, because she loved
> her, decided to let us become her new parents and
> love and care for her.
>
> "We love your/our daughter very much -- and
> we love you."

Michele commented later:

> I think Sharon helped me get myself together.
> I know she's OK where she is. We had our time
> together, and now I must get on with my life.

Michele graduated from high school four months after
the adoption. She has a job she enjoys, and a new boy
friend. They're getting married this winter.

Hector Fregoso, Children's Home Society social
worker, explained, "A single mother of a two- or three-
year-old usually has a much more difficult time deciding on
adoption than does a mother of a newborn. This is due in
part to family and peer pressures. She and her child have
shared many common experiences with them. These people

have a great deal of influence on her decision, and I think they should be supportive in whatever her choice may be.

"She has already spent many hours painfully considering her alternatives. She knows her child is growing, and has some needs she can't meet, especially if she's young and in the welfare cycle. She can't see a way out unless she remembers adoption."

MOTHER TOO SOON, SHE SAYS

Phyllis finds motherhood difficult. Her life with her small daughter is not satisfying. She shared her feelings:

I was living with my mother when I found I was pregnant. I didn't mean to get pregnant, but when it happened, I figured this would be a good way to get out of the house. My Mom and I weren't getting along at all then.

First Steve and I ran away to Eugene (Oregon), but I didn't like it there, so we came back and moved in with Steve's parents. That didn't work either, so two weeks before Heather was born, we got our own apartment.

Steve got a job, so I went off welfare -- but he was always getting fired. I didn't want to go back on welfare, and besides, I couldn't because I was living with Steve and he was working part of the time. But lots of times we didn't even have money for food. It was awful.

After Heather was born I lost contact with my friends. I see almost nobody, none of the people I used to hang around with before I had Heather. I don't really have friends I can go out with now, so I'm by myself most of the time. Steve was always out with his friends drinking beer and partying. I couldn't go with him because there was no one to watch Heather.

Finally I moved back with my Mom three months ago. Steve and I just weren't getting along. We still aren't. I had hoped my Mom would help me

out by watching Heather sometimes. But she tells
me she just got through raising kids -- she
doesn't have time now. Some girls like to stay
home and take care of a baby, but I think it's
hard. There's nobody I can even talk to that
really tells me how they feel. Everybody says
it's fun, it's great being a mother. I don't
agree.

Everybody was so nice to me when I was pregnant. They said, "Oh, I can't wait until you
have it. I'll babysit for you." Then as soon
as I had her, nobody seemed to care. They didn't
pay any attention at all to me and Heather any
more. It's hard finding somebody to babysit --
even when I have the money for it.

It's just no fun any more. Life is a drag.
There's nothing to live for but just to struggle.
People tell me I'm still young and have my whole
life ahead of me, but I want to have fun *now*.
It's routine every day -- I get up in the morning,
take Heather to school, go to school myself, then
come home and struggle with Heather.

"Did you ever consider adoption?"

Yes, when Heather was about five months old I thought about it. I talked to my Mom and she said, "Oh, you could never do something like that." She didn't seem to think at all about how I felt. She worried mostly about what other people would think. She said, "You made your mistake and you have to live with it!"

I still think about adoption, but I keep thinking it will be easier when she gets older. Maybe I can take care of her then. But I've been tied down since I was 16, and I haven't had time to do anything I want to do. All I can see ahead of me is problems. It's just too much responsibility for a young girl.

"How would you change your life if you could?"

Not have a child right now. Have a boy friend, somebody that cares about me. Just to have somebody. Having Heather limits me a lot with guys.

But if I gave Heather up, I wouldn't have anybody. I couldn't even go back to talk to my Mom. Everybody would look down on me and say, "How could you do that?"

I don't know whether I could do it -- give her up now. Of course I love her a lot, and sometimes I think she'd be better off with parents a little older and ready to settle down.

I don't know what to do.

SUSIE'S DECISION

Susie was (is) an adorable girl, very bright. Her large family was deeply involved in the Methodist Church. She had been a cheer leader at her high school.

Her family didn't like her boy friend at all. They were convinced he was a loser and that their daughter deserved better.

When Susie told her parents she was pregnant, they hit the roof. So she and Ed ran away. She was 16. She soon learned, to her disappointment, that Ed, too, was less than happy about the pregnancy. But they continued living together.

When she was about $7\frac{1}{2}$ months pregnant, Susie enrolled in the special class for pregnant students. She had passed her high school proficiency exam, but she decided to come to school because of the prepared childbirth instruction, prenatal health discussions, and the parenting class.

One day she commented:

I'm not sure I'm ready to be a mother, especially since Ed doesn't really want a baby. But I'll not decide until it's born.

Susie did decide to keep Letitia -- until she was nine months old. She finally decided at that time to give her daughter up for adoption.

A year later she shared her experiences with the students in the special class:

I feel giving up Letitia was the best possible decision for all of us. I'm still in contact with her and with her family. I know this is unusual, but for me, it's best. Especially now, during the holiday season, I have to know what is going on with her life.

People ask how I could do this, how I could give her up after being her mother for nine months. Well, I feel I was a very good mother, but I was able to put her in a home with a better atmosphere. I gave her to people who are raising her even better than I was.

It was like an answer to prayer the day my mother's friend called. I was feeling low, and I started talking to her. I was crying, and suddenly she said, "Susie, I know a family who might be interested in adopting Letitia. Let me call them and see how they feel." I told her to go ahead.

Two hours later she called me back and said, "These people want to meet you and Letitia, and they're interested in adopting her." Then she told me more about them. I had already heard of them through my Mom and Dad who knew them. They had two adopted children, five and eight years old.

Ed, Letitia, and I went over to see them. At that time Ed and I weren't getting along. He was not ready to be a father, and I thought our relationship was ending. I knew I didn't want to raise Letitia by myself.

We talked with them and with their children for hours. We were really impressed. They were down-to-earth people, family oriented, and they seemed super excited about taking Letitia. So we left her there that day and that night.

We went back each day for four days, and she seemed to be adjusting. It was hard for me. I would go home and cry and cry and think, I can't do this. But I had to bring myself to reality.

When you're pregnant, you get into kind of a fantasy world. You're not realistic. When I was pregnant, I "knew" things would work out with me and Ed. I "knew" my family would help me, and that it would get better. *But it really doesn't.* You just have to bring yourself back to reality before you can go ahead and make the decision that's best for you and for your baby.

Anyway, I left Letitia with this family and went to Albuquerque to be with my parents. I think that was the only way I could have left her. If I had stayed here, I simply wouldn't have been strong enough to do it.

A woman who lived across the street from my parents' home had relinquished a child several years earlier. We talked a lot and she helped me cope.

Three months later Letitia and her new family came to Albuquerque to visit. They let me take

care of Letitia for the whole weekend while they
visited friends there. She remembered me a little, and she was absolutely delightful, but she
obviously had a new family now.

Six months later I came back to Los Angeles.
Ed and I are together again and our relationship
is 1000 percent better. A lot of the pressure we
had felt between us was because of the baby. He
just wasn't ready to be a father, and I know now
I wasn't ready for parenthood either.

When I relinquished, I was a peer counselor
here in the Teen Mother Program. A lot of the
girls in my group got married. Only one other
girl relinquished. She went on to do the things
with her life that she wanted to do. Almost all
of the other girls ended up being stuck at home,
getting divorced, and being on welfare. I thought
then, and I still do, that I want more than that
for my baby and myself.

Most of the girls I know who have relinquished feel good about their decision. I tell
girls who are thinking of relinquishing that it's
going to hurt. It's going to hurt like Hell.
I'm not a crier, not especially emotional. When
it comes down to pain, I hold it in. But I think
it's important to let people know where you're
at.

Sometimes people think if you're going to
relinquish, you aren't going to think about it.
If you don't think about it, it will go away.
But it's not like that. It's with you for your
whole life. If the baby isn't with you physically, she's in your mind. I think about Letitia
every day, and that's like the other birth mothers
I know who have relinquished a child.

There is a complete cycle of grief you must
go through. I don't think you ever finish until
you go ahead and have a wanted baby. When you
start the mothering process and you aren't able

to finish it, the cycle isn't complete.

I saw Letitia a month ago on Halloween. She's 1½ now, and is just a doll. Her Mom is a total homemaker. She cooks and sews and does a lot of things I don't do, and she and I have a good relationship.

I met Letitia's grandparents too. You know, if I had kept her, she wouldn't have all these neat relationships with her brother and sister and with her grandparents. I think this is terribly important. I never knew my grandparents.

When you think about parents who are adopting, wow! They're really into it.

You can give your baby as much love as you have, but if you haven't finished growing up yet, that love can never be as much as your baby could

have from someone who has been waiting several
years for her.

I feel that if you have a child before you've
grown up yourself, it's going to be different. No
matter how much you think it's going to be OK,
that it will be like every other kid, it simply
isn't that way. There is still a social stigma
against children born to young single mothers.

You'll have some negative feelings and so
will other people. I think the child picks up on
this. If you keep the baby, this may affect her
whole life.

I feel keeping is sometimes a really selfish
decision. When you do this, you aren't thinking
about the future. You're thinking about what is
easier for you. . .it's not really easier to keep,
but relinquishing is a more difficult *decision* to
make.

This was the hardest thing I have ever done
in my life. But with anything you do, if it's
easy, it won't give you peace of mind. If it's
hard, and you know it's right, it will make you
feel *good*!

Four young women who became mothers too soon —
sooner than they wanted. Lorraine – Michele – Phyllis –
Susie. Phyllis is still agonizing over her future — and her
daughter's.

Lorraine – Michele – Susie – each faced the heartbreak of giving up the child she loved dearly. Each decided
she couldn't cope with motherhood at this point in her life.

Lorraine – Michele – Susie – each realized when
things got rough, she still had a choice. Adoption was still
an option for her child.

CHAPTER 10

Adoptees Grow Up

Were any of your friends adopted? Or do you know someone who adopted a child?

Many thousands of adoptions occur each year in the United States, and many of these adoptees are infants. More than 20,000 teenagers give up babies for adoption annually. You probably do know families with adopted children.

For many years most adoptive parents were extremely secretive about their child's adoption. Often the child was not told she was adopted. Novels are published dealing with the plight of the adolescent who suddenly learns she is not her parents' birth child. Research shows emotional problems often result from such situations.

But the problem generally was in the *secret,* not the adoption. How would you feel if, for sixteen years you assumed you were born to your parents, then accidentally learned you were adopted? The fact that your parents kept that information from you would probably hurt -- and hurt a lot. You might feel you couldn't trust them any more. If they hadn't been honest with you about something as basic as your birth, they must be dishonest in other things too.

But if dishonesty weren't involved, if you'd "always" known you were adopted, would it matter? If you had a good relationship with your parents, what difference would it make to you whether or not you were actually born to them? Twenty-four year old Janet sees no difference:

HEY, I'M ADOPTED!

I was three weeks old when I was adopted. I grew up in a very loving home and have never had any problem thinking of my parents as my parents. To me, they always have been. That's all I have known.

I can't tell you when I was first told I was adopted. My mom and I have a very open relationship, and we have talked about it a lot. It's as if I have always known. My mom said she and my dad made the decision to tell me before they adopted me because they thought it would be healthier for them and for me.

They had been married for ten years and had been trying to have a baby. Doctors couldn't find anything wrong with them, but they finally started proceedings to adopt. It took two years back then. They were told that if they didn't feel immediate bonding when they first saw me, not to take me. They felt it!

I have been raised as if I were very special. My mother told me I was a gift to them from God -- especially since there was no reason the doctor could find for them not conceiving and bearing children. By the time I was about two, she would bring adoption into our conversations. She used to read me stories about parents going to the hospital to *pick up* a baby, not to have it *born* there. Then she would tell me that was how they got me, that I didn't come from her tummy. I think it was this honesty that made me feel so good.

When I was in fourth or fifth grade I asked a lot of questions. About that time Mom also talked to me about menstruation and about the physicalness of having a baby. She always stressed that it was a very very hard thing that my natural parents did, giving me up. She was sure of this although she didn't know who they

were. She told me they must have loved me very much.

I went through some papers when I was in fifth grade, looking at stuff in the garage when my folks weren't home. I found the adoption papers and read about the physical characteristics of my parents. It said I was illegitimate so I raced into the house and got a dictionary -- I didn't know what it meant! The dictionary said it meant "bastard," and I knew that was bad so I started crying. Then my mom came home and I told her. She said that just meant they weren't married and that they wanted me to have a better home than they could give me. I thought that was OK.

When I was young, I wondered who they might be. Once I had a dream that my mother was Marilyn Monroe -- but that was only once! I was happy, and I never had any reason to think about it much.

Once I came across a big stack of sympathy cards in the garage. I felt awful, terribly jealous, because I figured Mom and Dad must have had another child. It took me about two weeks to get up enough nerve to ask my Mom. When I finally asked her, she laughed and hugged me, and said it was her father who passed away.

It was about that time I started asking if
she had ever been pregnant. She thinks she may
have been once, but she fell downstairs, then
did some very heavy bleeding.

When asked if she would like to find her birth parents, Janet replied:

For myself, I have really mixed feelings.
About one-fourth of me wants to do it and the
other three-fourths doesn't. I would be afraid
I might hurt Mom and Dad. I don't know if they
would care, but they have been so wonderful to
me that I don't know that I want to take the
risk.

If I did search, it would be simple curios-
ity -- seeing my birth parents in a room would
satisfy me, just having someone point them out
to me. I don't have a big desire to know more
about my roots.

There is one drawback to not knowing who
they are. I don't know whether my birth parents are now diabetic or have other illnesses.
It was after I was married that I was first
asked to fill out a family medical history, and
I couldn't do it! My parents were both tall
and I'm not. Neither is my husband. I'm wondering if we'll have tall children.

I have always accepted being adopted and I
have always been proud of it. When I was small,
I used to run up to people and say, "Hey, I'm
adopted!"

People used to ask me who my *real* parents
were. I always said I'm with my *real* parents.
They're all I've ever known. They're super,
and I doubt if I could have been happier in any
other situation.

It is a hard decision to give up a child --
and it takes a lot of love to make that decision.
Now that I'm older, I can see how difficult it

would be to go through pregnancy, then give up.

But if you put it in perspective and think about what would be best for the child so far as the future is concerned. . .I'm glad my birth parents loved me enough to let me go!

When she was considering releasing her baby for adoption, Lisa (Chapter Three) said she would try to imagine her baby in one of the adoptive homes described by her social worker. "Then I would think about my child being told later that he was adopted. I could imagine him thinking, "God, why would my Mom give me up for adoption?"

Janet obviously didn't feel like that. Neither did Donna, who is a 42 year old mother of three children:

DONNA REMEMBERS

I was adopted in an age when adoption was almost a shame. I realize now that taking an adopted child then was quite a step, and you didn't ever talk about it. You knew people knew, but you did not discuss it.

My parents didn't tell me I was adopted until I was about twelve, and the only reason they told me then was because I asked. I had heard it from someone else. A child I was baby sitting said something to me about my being adopted. That child didn't realize I didn't know. I couldn't believe it. I thought, should I ask my parents?

Then one day I came home from school and said to my mother, "Am I adopted?"

This look of horror came over her face and she said, "Where did you hear about this?"

"Someone at school told me," I said.

She said, "I don't want to talk about it."

Then three nights later she and my dad sat

down and told me all about it.

Then I asked about my sister Betty. They said she was adopted too. I said to my mother, "It really doesn't matter, does it, because you love me?" I had to reassure her! My parents loved me and my sister dearly. They always have and they always will.

About a year ago my dad said, "We wanted children so badly and we had our names in for a boy and a girl. About three years after we had our first girl we got a call that they had another baby, but it was a girl. We went in the next day, and your mother was so excited she wouldn't let anyone else hold you."

I had never heard that before. I wish they had told me that story when I was twelve. It would have meant even more to me then than it does now.

I have never had that tremendous urge to know about my biological background. But when I started having children, I thought perhaps I should find out. So I wrote a letter to Children's Home Society and told them I was married, having children of my own, and any information they could give me on my hereditary background would be helpful.

They sent back a delightful letter, but without names. My mother was a sixteen year old high school girl. My father was a little older, out of high school, a laborer. My mother was just unable to support me. They told me I was mostly Irish with a little German and Dutch mixed in. There were no hereditary diseases.

They wrote, "Both parents were people of innate refinement." It was probably a stock phrase, but to anyone 23 years old, it's kind of nice to think your birth parents were not uncouth boors. I have never pursued it any further.

To whomever gave me up I am grateful because
I can't imagine that my life could have been any
better than being with my adoptive parents.
They were the kind of parents I would have chosen if I had a choice.

When asked how she would feel if her birth mother
looked for her, Donna said thoughtfully:

I wouldn't mind.   The only thing that might bother me is if it hurt my adoptive parents.   I would
probably say, "Thank you for giving me up," because I was very much wanted and very much loved.
I think that is the greatest thing you can give
your child.

Actually, I think it would be better if my
birth parents came to me instead of the other way
around.   They couldn't disrupt my life because
I'm too secure.   But can you imagine appearing on
a birth mother's doorstep 42 years later?   What
would happen then?"

Not learning she was adopted until she was twelve
may have been the norm thirty years ago when Donna was a
child. Today, however, adoptive parents are much more apt
to follow Janet's mother's example and tell their children
very early that they are adopted.

Cathy Warner, Children's Home Society counselor,
mentioned that they insist that adoptive parents agree to be
open with their children about the adoption. One adoptive
family also reported that the judge, in their final hearing,
"made" them promise to tell their son he was adopted.

Jane and Donna each had warm feelings about her
birth parents. Each evidenced some, but not overwhelming,
desire to meet them. Janet was concerned about hurting her
adoptive parents, while Donna worried that she might disrupt her birth mother's life if she searched for her.

What "search rights" should adult adoptees have?

Adult Adoptees' Rights

Several books have been published recently about adult adoptees searching for their parents. Adoptees have organized to "fight" for their right to learn about their biological background. It is hard to learn how the majority of adoptees feel. The question can be compared to any individual's attitudes toward learning about his/her family "tree." Some people go to great lengths to trace their "roots" while others aren't interested.

Adoptees' wishes on the matter of searching for birth parents differ too. A father discussed the difference between his two grown children, an adopted son and an adopted daughter:

My son wanted desperately to find his birth mother. After much searching, he did find her and was pleased to learn she was a nice person. She gave him a lot of family background about his genetic parents and grandparents. This answered a lot of the questions he had had for many years.

He says this has helped him understand why he reacts to certain situations in one way although his life with us would seemingly cause him to react in different ways. He also says that he feels closer to my wife and me than he ever has, that finding his birth mother actually improved our relationship!

On the other hand, my daughter, also adopted, has shown no interest in finding her birth parents.

Adoptees' Opinions Researched

Children's Home Society of California in 1976 published "The Changing Face of Adoption." This was a magazine devoted to the question of what rights, if any, adopted adults have to information that was "sealed" when their adoption was approved by the court.

Included in the magazine were questionnaires to be answered and returned to the CHS research department by adult adoptees, birth parents, and adoptive parents. Three-hundred nine adult adoptees returned completed questionnaires, most of them from California. Eighteen sent letters with their questionnaires.

Results of the research were published in 1977 by Children's Home Society: "The Changing Face of Adoption, Report of Research Project."

Apparently most adult adoptees feel they can discuss their adoption with their parents. Almost three-fourths of those completing the questionnaire said they were either "totally" or "usually" comfortable doing so. The younger the adoptee, the easier it was for her/him to discuss adoption with the parents.

"Are you satisfied with the information you have about your birth parents?" was also asked. Almost half were either "totally" or "generally" satisfied. Adoptees had gotten

most of their information from their adoptive parents and the adoption agency. A few had received information directly from their birth parents.

About two-thirds of the adoptees wanted more information. They wished to have biological data (nationality, medical, hereditary diseases, etc.), current facts about their birth parents and possible brothers and sisters. They also expressed personal concern, wondering why they were released for adoption.

Of the 309 adoptees in the CHS survey, almost one-third had thought "all the time" or "often" about searching for their birth parents. Another quarter thought about it occasionally, while the rest said they never considered searching.

These adoptees were also asked why they did or did not want to search for their parents. Those who wanted to find their birth parents gave three major reasons:

1. Biological. They wondered if they resembled their birth parents. They wanted to know their health history. They wondered if they had brothers and sisters.

2. Identity. They felt part of their identity was missing. They wanted to know why their parents released them for adoption.

3. Parent Now/Peace of Mind. A few people wrote, "Because I am a parent now, I want my birth parents to know everything is all right. I want to give them peace of mind."

Ninety-eight of the adoptees said they had tried to find their birth parents. Thirty-four had made contact and an additional eight knew where they were but hadn't yet contacted them.

Adoptees' comments were overwhelmingly positive. They reported a wide range of responses from a single telephone contact to frequent visits. One wrote:

I found my birth mother in June and visited her in August. I probably couldn't have done it without the help of my adoptive parents.

don't think it was easy for them but they gave
me their understanding and they also sent me a
check to pay for my trip out to Utah to meet my
birth mother.

My birth mother had felt that it was "not her
place" to try to find me -- I think she felt she
didn't deserve to meet me -- but when I first
called her, she said, "I thought this might happen. It's wonderful. Would you like to come
visit me?" I feel great about having met her and
am planning to spend my 28th birthday with her
this summer. I have never been as close as I am
now to my adoptive parents.

"If your birth parents indicated a wish to contact you,
would you want the agency or other intermediary to let you
know?" was another question. More than three out of four
of the adoptees said yes, but many of them wanted agency
help in setting up such a meeting. Almost half, however,
said they would be pleased if their birth parents contacted
them directly.

Further research of adult adoptees, birthparents, and
adoptive parents is reported in *The Adoption Triangle: The
Effects of the Sealed Record on Adoptees, Birth Parents, and Adoptive Parents* by Sorosky, Baran, and
Pannor.

An Adoptee Comments

Donna expressed feelings much like those of the other
adult adoptees I interviewed. I asked her if she had any
comments for a 15-year-old whose baby will soon be born,
a baby she plans to release for adoption. She replied:

The love that her adoptive parents will have
for your child will be as great as the love you
have for her -- not necessarily greater, but
certainly just as great. I really believe that
the greatest love a 15- or 16-year-old can have
for her baby is to give her up *unless* she can get
all kinds of support from her family. A baby gets

twice as much love if it has a father to relate to all the time.

From my own experience, I received so much
from my adoptive parents that I am eternally
grateful to my birth mother for what she gave
to me.

CHAPTER 11

Adoptive Parents' Experiences

The following item appeared recently in the *Des Moines Register:*

> I stayed with my parents for several days after the birth of our first child. One afternoon I remarked to my mother that it was surprising our baby had dark hair since both my husband and I are fair. She said, "Well, your daddy has black hair."
>
> "But, Mama, that doesn't matter because I'm adopted."
>
> With an embarrassed smile she said the most wonderful words I've ever heard: "I always forget." (Rodessa E. Morris, Gladys, Va.)

What are adoptive parents like? Are they really "normal" people?

Or perhaps you've read a novel about a poor little orphan taken in by cold, unloving parents? And she's supposed to be grateful for everything they've done for her!

You can be sure those cold parents weren't "real." That story about the poor little orphan is about as fictional as you can get. Real life adoptive parents are apt to be even warmer and more loving than some birth families. . .

perhaps because they've waited so long for their children.

With thousands of babies relinquished for adoption each year in the United States, of course adoptive parents vary a great deal. Birth parents aren't alike either. Families show a great deal of variety. But adoptive families tend to be similar in one characteristic -- they love their children very much -- just as nearly all birth parents do.

An adoptive mother commented:

We moved to California because we had heard good things about adoption out here. The first thing we did was call Children's Home Society. They sent us a form which invited us to go to a meeting with other people wanting to adopt a child.

It was a room full of people (really only 20), and the case worker told us there weren't enough children for all of us. But if we could stick out the selection process, she said we might have a child.

First we each wrote an autobiography. The case worker visited us at home several times and we were updated quarterly as to what our situation was. We adopted Erin nine days after she was born. She's been such a joy to us.

Sometimes I feel a little guilty about the closeness I feel for her because I didn't have quite that much with our other children. We have two others and I thought I was close to them. But there is a magnetism with Erin that is really something. She has me wrapped around her little finger and I love it. . .I love it!

We have a really positive feeling about Erin's other mother. She's in college and didn't feel she was ready yet to be a mother.

JOHNSON FAMILY DESCRIBED

Now consider the Johnsons, a family with adopted children. Susan and Steve have four children: Eric, 17; Bill, 15; Pat, 13; and Barbara, 10.

Tall and dark haired, Eric is a high achiever at school. He works hard, is rather quiet, and has earned a scholarship to a good university next year.

Stocky Bill is into athletics. He was active in Little League and has won several district awards through his high school swim team activities. He doesn't spend much time on his studies -- he's too busy with sports and handling his paper route.

Blond, freckled Pat is also an athlete. She was a Bobby Sox All Star team member this year, is a strong player on her school's basketball team, and is an active participant in track events. She is also active in her church youth group.

Barbara plays the piano well, likes school, but considers athletics to be harder work than she wants. She's apt to offer to help her mother fix dinner, especially if she can make the dessert.

The Johnson children have very different talents, interests, and achievements. Perhaps it's because they're all adopted?

No, that's not the reason -- Bill and Eric were adopted, but Pat and Barbara were born to Susan and Steve. Susan shared their story:

We only expected the two boys, and you can imagine how surprised we were when I became pregnant the first time. Then, two years after Pat was born, another miracle -- I was pregnant again! We couldn't believe our good fortune. . . a family of four children when at one time we thought we might not have any! If I had it to do over and could choose, I would do exactly the same thing -- adopt Eric and Bill, then give birth to Pat and Barbara.

I really believe these kids are all gifts from God. I think once you adopt them, they're yours. . .in every respect, completely, just as if you had them by birth.

People have often said that Eric looks exactly like his dad -- he even walks like him. When he was little, he was a born mimic. It's interesting that Eric looks more like Steve than either of our birth children does.

We know Bill's mother had musical talents, and we have seen it in him almost from the beginning. But I can't get him to take lessons. He did play the piano for a few years, but he's just too busy with baseball to think about it now.

Several years ago when Bill was in grade school, a symphony orchestra came to school.

They had every percussion instrument there is and
he got so excited. At that time he was going to
be a drummer. . .he did play drums two years in
junior high. But now it's all sports.

When we decided we wanted to adopt a child,
we went to an agency. But we were told we had
to wait until we were married five years. Then
our doctor asked if we wanted to adopt independently. We decided to go ahead. We had been
told we couldn't have children by birth.

The social worker from the county came quite
a few times to check us out, sometimes early in
the morning! She was nice but I was always a
little nervous. She'd sit and talk, and she usually wanted to see the children's rooms. She
checked our bank statements occasionally. It
took a year for each adoption to become final.
Sometimes we'd worry, but mostly we just went
along loving the kids.

At first we wondered how to tell them they
were adopted. Then someone suggested we mention
the word occasionally, and that's what we did.
If I saw a friend while I was out shopping, for
instance, I'd say, "We just adopted this beautiful baby." We sent out announcements that they
were adopted. We never did have to sit down and
tell them -- they knew and accepted it.

I also told them about their mothers, that
each mother had thought it would be better for
her son to have another family.

I've often wondered what their birth mothers
are thinking on their birthdays. Of course they
think of them. . .that's only normal!

I've asked both Eric and Bill if they're interested in finding their birth parents. We
have their names and addresses at the time of
birth. Bill several years ago asked me what his
name would have been and I told him, but he has

never mentioned it since. Perhaps they'll want
to search later.

Pat sometimes resents the fact that she isn't
adopted! I think she said something about it
when Eric was critically ill. That's the time
you know *absolutely* they're your own kids whether they're yours by adoption or by birth.
You *know* there is no difference whatsoever.

The Johnsons are unusual in that they had two more
children by birth after they had adopted two. A major reason for a couple adopting a child, of course, is because
they are infertile (can't get pregnant for some reason).
Only about five percent of these couples have a child (or
children) by birth after they adopt.

The Johnsons' story, unique as it is, is a reassuring
answer to that age-old question, "If someone else adopts
my baby, would they really treat/love her as their very
own?"

ONLY CHILD IS ADOPTED

The Washingtons have only one child. They had
hoped to adopt a second baby but the agency had very few
babies available for placement when they applied. The infants they did have, the social worker explained, would be
placed with couples who had no children.

Marge and Earl Washington's son, Ralph, is twelve.
He was six weeks old when they adopted him. Marge described their family:

Our caseworker called one day and said, "We
have a baby, a little boy. Come over and see
him and let us know if you're interested." I
was teaching then, and I had gotten her call
after school. So I picked Earl up from work,
and we drove over. He was the most beautiful
baby we had ever seen, and to our amazement,
they let us take him home right then! We were
delighted.

I quit my teaching job that same day. We had applied a year earlier and had been told about ten months later that we had "passed" the home visits. But we had also been told the wait might be as long as two years. We don't know why we were called so soon. . .we never asked!

We had a room for him but not much else. Our neighbors came through with a crib and an infant seat. Earl made a quick trip to the store for bottles, formula, and diapers. You can imagine how excited we were.

We had decided to adopt simply because we wanted a child. We had several friends who had

WE COULD NEVER HAVE A CHILD *UNLESS* SOMEONE WAS WILLING TO GIVE UP FOR ADOPTION. . .

adopted, and we knew it "worked." We'd been married seven years, and I just couldn't get pregnant. Doctors told us I wouldn't be able to have
a child of my own -- but we do -- Ralph is our
own.

In my own family it was no big deal. I had
one brother who was a bit skeptical about adoption, but when I put Ralph on his lap, that ended
that!

A friend in the throes of morning sickness
during her pregnancy once said ruefully that maybe adoption is the easy way to go. I told her
that, while I was concerned that she didn't feel
well that day, adoption wasn't so easy either.
I think if all parents had to go through the
soul searching and the questioning that we did
with the agency, many might not be parents today!

The Washingtons live in a beautiful home near the
mountains. It's a neighborhood deeply involved in Little
League, scouting, and PTA activities. According to Marge
and Earl, a surprising number of children in their neighborhood are adopted. Marge, who often works as a volunteer aide in Ralph's class at school, claims that at least
five children in each grade are adopted:

When we moved here, there were already three
families on our block with an adopted child, and
we made the fourth. When I learn that a play-
mate of Ralph's is adopted, I usually throw out
a comment to him so if they want to talk about
it, they can. But Earl says, "You know they
don't talk about adoption. All those kids talk
about is baseball, 'Star Wars,' whatever, but
certainly not adoption!"

We talked to Ralph about his adoption from
the beginning. He seldom mentions it. But just
yesterday I was measuring him and marking his
height on the wall where we have his "growing
chart." I said, "Just look, Ralph, you weighed
only 7½ pounds when you were born, and now you

weigh 80."

He said, "Gee, do you suppose my real parents would be surprised?"

People ask us if we'll be upset if he wants to find his birth parents when he's grown. But we figure that when he's grown, he'll be his own man. I think he probably will. Some of his interests are much like his birth parents, and some day that may intrigue him.

I've told Ralph more than once that his birth mother must have had tremendous love for him to be able to give him up. I personally think that's about the biggest act of courage possible.

He asked me once why I thought his mother gave him to us. I told him it wasn't possible for her to care for him the way she wanted him cared for. She loved him so much she wanted to give him to someone who could take care of him as she wanted.

Marge and Earl Washington don't worry about Ralph contacting his birth mother. They know their love for Ralph -- and his love for them -- would not be threatened. In fact, they compare it to the parents-in-law ties he will probably have some day. They concluded: "We have enough love for each other -- surely we won't be jealous of his other relationships."

ADOPTIVE PARENTS SURVEYED

But how do adoptive couples generally feel about their children "searching" for their birth parents? Almost 1,000 adoptive parents answered a questionnaire on the subject from Children's Home Society of California in 1976.

Most of them had adopted their children through an agency, and most of the children were adopted as infants. Almost all (95%) of the adoptive parents had told their child/children by age six that they were adopted. About two-thirds of the adoptive parents reported their children had asked many questions about their birth parents. The

majority of the adoptive parents wished they had more information about their children's birth parents.

Adoptive parents' feelings are often listed as the reason for maintaining secrecy in adoptions. Yet two-thirds
of these respondents said they would feel totally comfortable or "more-or-less comfortable" if their child did search
for his birth parents. The more recent the placement of the
child in their home, the more positive were the adoptive
parents' feelings toward such a search.

Adoptive parents were asked, "How would you feel if
the birth parent of your adult child contacted you, or the
adoptee, seeking reunion?" Respondents were divided three
ways -- about one-third felt very positive about the idea,
one-third was more-or-less comfortable, and the other one-
third thought they would be upset at such a contact.

The CHS survey also involved birth parents and
adults who were adopted. Most people, whether they are
birth parents, adoptive parents, or adult adoptees, seem
most concerned about respecting the wishes of the other
people making up their "adoption triangle." Many adoptive
parents, as related above, feel comfortable with the idea
that their child might meet his/her birth parents some day.

The adoptees described in this book are interested
in meeting their birth parents *if* their birth parents would
want a reunion. They do not want such a reunion, however,
if it might upset their birth parents' lives.

But the question of open versus sealed adoption records may not matter to you now. What does matter is your
baby's family -- whether the family is you or an adoptive
couple. If you choose to release for adoption, the important
thing now is the love and care the adoptive parents will give
your child.

Be assured that adoptive parents can indeed give
your son or daughter as much love and as satisfying a family life as if s/he were born to them. Witness the Johnson
and Washington families!

APPENDIX

QUESTIONNAIRE

AM I PARENT MATERIAL?

(The following questionnaire is provided by the National Alliance for Optional Parenthood.)

Here are some questions for you to consider before you deal with the important decision of whether or not to have a child.

If you decide to have a child, it'll be a decision that will affect you for the rest of your life. Thank about it. Taking responsibility for a new life is awesome.

These questions are designed to raise ideas that you may not have thought about. There are no "right" answers and no "grades" –– your answers are "right" for you and may help you decide for youself whether or not you want to be a parent. Because we all change, your answers to some of these questions may change two, five, even ten years from now.

You *do* have a choice. Check out what you know and give it some thought. Then do what seems right for you.

DOES HAVING AND RAISING A CHILD FIT THE LIFESTYLE I WANT?

1. What do I want out of life for myself? What do I think is important?

2. Could I handle a child and a job at the same time? Would I have time and energy for both?

3. Would I be ready to give up the freedom to do what I want to do, when I want to do it?

4. Would I be willing to cut back my social life and spend more time at home? Would I miss my free time and privacy?

5. Can I afford to support a child? Do I know how much it takes to raise a child?

6. Do I want to raise a child in the neighborhood where I live now? Would I be willing and able to move?

7. How would a child interfere with my growth and development?

8. Would a child change my educational plans? Do I have the energy to go to school and raise a child at the same time?

9. Am I willing to give a great part of my life -- AT LEAST 18 YEARS -- to being responsible for a child? And spend a large portion of my life being concerned about my child's well being?

WHAT'S IN IT FOR ME?

1. Do I like doing things with children? Do I enjoy activities that children can do?

2. Would I want a child to be "like me"?

3. Would I try to pass on to my child my ideas and values? What if my child's ideas and values turn out to be different from mine?

4. Would I want my child to achieve things that I wish I had, but didn't?

5. Would I expect my child to keep me from being lonely in my old age? Do I do that for my parents? Do my parents do that for my grandparents?

6. Do I want a boy or a girl child? What if I don't get what I want?

7. Would having a child show others how mature I am?

8. Will I prove I am a man or a woman by having a child?

9. Do I expect my child to make my life happy?

Raising a child? What's there to know?

1. Do I like children? When I'm around children for a while, what do I think or feel about having one around all of the time?

2. Do I enjoy teaching others?

3. Is it easy for me to tell other people what I want, or need, or what I expect of them?

4. Do I want to give a child the love (s)he needs? Is loving easy for me?

5. Am I patient enough to deal with the noise and the confusion and the 24-hour-a-day responsibility? What kind of time and space do I need for myself?

6. What do I do when I get angry or upset? Would I take things out on a child if I lost my temper?

7. What does discipline mean to me? What does freedom, or setting limits, or giving space mean? What is being too strict, or not strict enough? Would I want a perfect child?

8. How do I get along with my parents? What will I do to avoid the mistakes my parents made?

9. How would I take care of my child's health and safety? How do I take care of my own?

10. What if I have a child and find out I made a wrong decision?

Have my partner and I really talked about becoming parents?

1. Does my partner want to have a child? Have we talked about our reasons?

2. Could we give a child a good home? Is our relationship a happy and strong one?

3. Are we both ready to give our time and energy to raising a child?

4. Could we share our love with a child without jealousy?

5. What would happen if we separated after having a child,

or if one of us should die?

6. Do my partner and I understand each other's feelings about religion, work, family, child raising, future goals? Do we feel pretty much the same way? Will children fit into these feelings, hopes and plans?

7. Suppose one of us wants a child and the other doesn't? Who decides?

8. Which of the questions in this pamphlet do we need to *really* discuss before making a decision?

GOOD LUCK IN MAKING YOUR DECISION, AND GOOD WISHES FOR A HAPPY AND FULFILLED FUTURE.

This paper was prepared by Carole Baker, Executive Director of the National Alliance for Optional Parenthood, in cooperation with Elizabeth K. Canfield, Health and Family Planning Counselor, University of Southern California; Dr. Robert E. Gould, Professor of Psychiatry, New York Medical College; Dr. E. James Lieberman, Associate Clinical Professor of Psychiatry, George Washington University School of Medicine; Angel Martinez, Director of Special Projects, James Bowman Associates, San Francisco; and Dr. Burleigh Seaver, Research Associate, Pennsylvania State University, Institute for Research on Human Resources.

Additional copies of "AM I PARENT MATERIAL?" are available from the National Alliance for Optional Parenthood, 2010 Massachusetts Ave., NW, Washington, D.C. 20036. 2-49, 10¢ each; 50-199, 9¢ each; 200-499, 8¢ each; 500 or more, 7¢ each. Available in Spanish.

If Your Daughter is Pregnant

Ideally, parents of a pregnant teenager will support her during her pregnancy and afterward in whatever decision she makes. It is their daughter who will experience the intense feelings of approaching motherhood. It is *she* who will suffer the pain of losing her baby if she does decide to relinquish.

If she keeps her baby, it is *she* who will (should) take the responsibility of parenting -- first a tiny infant, then a toddler, preschooler, and on until her child reaches adulthood some eighteen years later. The baby won't be her parents' responsibility (although some grandparents do assume the role of parenting the baby).

"Parental pressure to keep is overwhelming," commented Charlotte De Armond, Public Affairs Director for Children's Home Society of California.

"So often it's 'my grandchild' we're talking about, without much thought as to whether or not a 15 year old mother is best for that grandchild," she continued. "Sometimes, too, the teenager's mother is getting to the age when she can't have her own baby so she wants to have this one."

"I have never known a girl who gave up her baby at birth if her parents wanted her to keep it," Cathy Warner, CHS social worker, reported, "but it does go the other way -- I've known several girls whose parents wanted them to give the baby up, but they didn't."

The young women who share their lives in this book often commented, "My Mom said she would stand by me in whatever decision I made." That was important to them. Several girls who released their babies for adoption mentioned mothers who wanted a grandchild, but who realized this was not a reason for their daughter to keep her baby,

Eva placed her baby for adoption four years ago. She wasn't living with her mother while she was pregnant, but her friends kept telling her she should keep her baby. She explained:

That was the hardest. But if you keep because your friends want you to, that's not a good reason!

Now, four years later, I know I didn't make a mistake. I gave life to someone who wanted it. People have said to me, "I couldn't give my baby up. I would feel guilty." Well, I would feel guilty if I hadn't given her up. My mother would be raising her because I have to work -- and I don't want a child who sees me only an hour each night and who thinks she is my mother's daughter!

It must have been difficult for my mother. The day after the baby was born she stayed with me. She held the baby, and I know it was hard for her -- she had five kids, and this was her first grandchild. But she never told me what I should do -- she left it all up to me.

Holding her in my arms in the hospital was the hardest part of making that decision. But I just looked at her and told her it was for her I was doing this. I know I could have been a good mother, but I couldn't give her the home I wanted for her.

I have a friend who had a son when she was 16. She thought about adoption, but her mother was horrified. "You can't give up *our* baby," she said.

So my friend now has a three year old son.
At 19, she's tied down to a full-time job, a job
she hates. She's given up (at 19!) most of the
dreams she had for her life.

SOME PARENTS PUSH ADOPTION

Susan had a different goal. She desperately wanted
a child. Her parents, however, were determined that she
not become a mother yet.

"We have a student who wants to talk to you.
Can you come over this morning?" The caller was
a counselor from a neighboring high school.

Thirty minutes later I met Susan. I soon
learned she was the girl I had heard about the
previous week. She was pregnant and her folks
were insisting she get an abortion.

Susan, close to tears, started talking.

"My parents can't stand Carlos -- they think
that because his parents don't speak English and
aren't rich, they don't amount to anything. But
I love him!" she wailed. We talked for an hour.
Susan told me about her family, her relationship
with Carlos, and how she didn't want an abortion.

I heard a few days later that Susan had run
away from home and was living with Carlos and his
parents. Four days later she was home, and the
next day her parents took her to the hospital for
an abortion. (Illegal? Only if Susan didn't sign
the release form. Parents have no legal right to
insist their daughter get an abortion, but from a
realistic standpoint, it can -- and does -- happen.)

less than a year later Susan was in my class.
She was pregnant again, but she was no longer with
Carlos. Because of her parents, they had split up
after she had the abortion. Now she was pregnant

by someone else, a boy she scarcely knew and insisted she didn't care about. By the time she
told her parents, it was too late for another
abortion.

When I visited her home after she had enrolled in the class, Susan excused herself. Her
mother and I talked. Mrs. Lacey was a lovely,
well-groomed woman in her late 40s, perhaps 50s.
She had three married children who lived nearby.
She worked for an insurance agency.

"We just don't understand," she said tear-
fully. "We've done everything for Susan, and
look what's happened. We were terribly hurt
last year when she was involved with that worth-
less boy -- and his family made no attempt to
stop them. We were relieved when that was over
-- we could start again. We told Susan we
wouldn't hold that against her. If she would
work hard in school and do her best to get along
at home, we'd never mention that mess.

"And we thought things were going pretty
well. Then three weeks ago she sprang this on
us. And this time she doesn't even care about
the boy! We can't believe it. And she wants to
keep the baby. . .

"But we've told her she can't bring a baby
back here. If she keeps that baby, she'll have
to live some place else. She says she would
take care of it, but I know better. I know how
she doesn't take responsibility. I know I'd
end up having that baby, and I've already had
my family. That part of my life is gone, and I
don't want to start over."

Susan continued coming to school, but she
seemed more and more depressed as the weeks went
by. At first she had told me how much she wanted this baby, that no one could talk her out of
keeping it. She was still hoping she could live
at home after her baby's birth.

But about a month before delivery she admitted to herself that her parents meant it. She really couldn't go home with her baby. And she decided she wasn't ready to survive by herself. Her parents talked to their lawyer, and an independent adoption was arranged.

Susan delivered a little boy one cold February night. She said she didn't want to see her son. She signed the consent for release from the hospital, and the baby was placed immediately with his new family.

Susan returned to her other school. She graduated from high school in June. A few months later she called to tell me she was pregnant again. "And this time I'm finally going to have a baby of my own," she told me.

Those two years were difficult times for Susan. She will always remember the two children she doesn't have -- the one she lost unwillingly through abortion, and the other through adoption. Apparently there was no "good" solution to the conflict between her desire to have a child and her parents' determination that she not become a mother at 16.

Susan's case is not unusual. Statistics show a high pregnancy repeat rate among girls who feel they are pushed into either abortion or adoption against their wishes.

Her story also highlights another fairly common occurrence -- parents who know they don't want another child to care for. It seems harsh, but this also means their daughter won't have the heavy problem of trying to cope with a baby who has two mothers -- his own and his grandmother. A child needs *one* mother, not two.

SOME PARENTS PUSH KEEPING

Gina is an unhappy school dropout at age 16 because her mother, unlike Susan's, insisted she keep her baby. After all, that was her grandchild. . .

Gina's mother told me indignantly that several people had said Gina should give up her baby for adoption. Because Gina was 14½ and had some learning problems, her social worker and her school counselor had each urged the family to consider relinquishment.

"But that's her baby and no way would I want her to give it up," her mother said vehemently. "We'll all help her. Besides, I'll enjoy having a baby around here again."

Gina had a little girl. A month later she returned to her special class for educationally handicapped youngsters at her high school. Her mother would care for her baby while she was in school.

The following semester, however, Gina's counselor called to ask if Gina could transfer to our high school. She needed the Infant Center, he said. I asked about the mother. "She's tired of baby sitting," he replied. "She told Gina that baby is her responsibility and she has to find a way to take care of her."

But our school had no class for the educationally handicapped. Because of her problems, Gina couldn't enroll. So she dropped out of school to care for her baby -- the baby for whom adoption was unthinkable because Gina's mother said, "Of course we'll keep her."

OTHERS LET DAUGHTER DECIDE

But some parents realize it is far better to encourage their teenage daughter to make her own decision. Sometimes that decision is to keep the baby, sometimes to release -- and the decision the young mother makes may not be the same decision her parents would make.

Robin shared her story in Chapter Two. She is 19 and her son, Stu, is 3½. Robin copes beautifully with the hard work as well as the joys of being a young single

mother. Perhaps part of her success is due to her own
mother:

> "I understand this must be Robin's responsi-
> bility," her mother said. She and Robin had come
> in to learn about the special class. But Mrs.
> Trevino, while she appeared interested, obviously
> wasn't going to decide for Robin about school.
>
> More important, neither was she going to at-
> tempt to decide something as crucial as whether
> Robin at 15 would actually become a mother. She
> had urged her daughter to check out adoption, had
> even made the appointment with the counselor for
> her, and provided transportation.
>
> She did consider it important that Robin make
> a *choice,* her own choice. She didn't want her
> daughter to stumble into parenting simply because
> she was now pregnant.

Jodie's mother (Chapter Three) also stressed that
whatever decision Jodie made was the "right one." She
would help her cope, but she wouldn't be a live-in baby sit-
ter:

> Mrs. Foster thought Jodie would keep her baby.
> She had assured Jodie, however, that she would
> support whatever decision she made. About a month
> before delivery, Jodie decided to relinquish. She
> also decided she didn't want to see her baby. But
> because she delivered December 23, she couldn't
> reach her adoption worker before she went home on
> Christmas Day. So she took her baby with her and
> cared for him for two days before giving him up.
>
> Her mother had supported her in her late adop-
> tion plans. Then she had helped her when she took
> the baby home. Jodie had not talked to the social
> worker when her mother left for work two days af-
> ter Christmas.
>
> When she came home and found the baby gone,
> she said, "I didn't think you could do it." But
> it was an accepting comment. It really *was*

Jodie's decision.

Two years later Jodie commented:

"I look at my life now and I think how different it could have been. I have several friends who are single mothers. One is still living at home with her mother.

"She has to work, so her mother quit her job to take care of the baby. There is constant conflict between them. Their ideas about discipline are very different, and they're always disagreeing on how to raise that child.

"I think of where I would be," she continued. "Last year I worked fourteen days straight before Christmas. There would have been no possible way for me to celebrate my son's birthday with him."

Jodie is very active in her church. She leads a youth group, sings in the choir, and has taken several trips with these groups. "I think I'm more capable of serving the Lord now than I would be as a single parent," she mused. "I wonder if I would resent my baby if I had kept him. Would I sometimes be ashamed to say, 'This is my child' just as sometimes now I'm ashamed to say I was a teen mother?

"One woman at church had tried especially hard to talk me into keeping my child," she remembered. "She was dead set against adoption, and she made that perfectly clear to me.

"But the other day she came up to me, put her arm around me, and said, 'You know, I realize now how right you were in your decision to give up your baby. I look at my life -- I married because I was pregnant. I see where I am now, how my life is going. Then I look at yours, and think how my life could have been. I'm sorry I tried to talk you out of it.'

"I hugged her," Jodie said simply.

WHAT IS RATIONAL?

It is indeed a fine line between "supporting" someone
in *her* decision versus applying pressure for her to follow
your wishes. Attempts at being "rational" can be difficult.
After all, what is "rational" about a mother giving up her
baby? On the other hand, what is "rational" about a tenth
grader assuming the role of motherhood?

In our society, there are extreme risks either way.
There is the risk of real emotional trauma for the young
birth mother if she releases her baby for adoption. There
are risks of no job skills, not enough education, no time to
have fun for the teenager who chooses too-early parenthood.

So what's a parent to do?

No one can tell you what is best in your situation.
Was Susan's mother wrong absolutely to forbid her daughter
to bring the baby home? Would Mrs. Lacey have been "right"
if she had decided to help Susan cope with motherhood by
taking over the responsibility for her grandchild? No, Mrs.
Lacey was quite right to insist that she had had her family
and she didn't want another one. That was *her* decision to
make, not her daughter's.

But Susan might have fared better if she had had a
chance to look at her options, to make a choice based on
what was possible in her family. She had no one excepting
herself to care for a baby. Could she have coped? Possibly.
Possibly not.

Discussing her situation with a trained adoption counselor might have helped Susan look at her various alternatives. Instead, her family simply called their lawyer to set
up the adoption.

Accepting Susan's blythe "I can take care of it -- I
love babies" might not be practical. Encouraging her to
"try" could be very hard on her baby. If she found she
couldn't cope, the trauma of releasing that baby later would
have been even greater than it was at birth.

Jim Mead, founder of For Kids Sake, Inc., an organization devoted to the prevention of child abuse, has a unique

suggestion for parents trying to toilet train their toddler. He recommends they "rent a kid" for a weekend. The requirement is that the "rented kid" will take that toddler with him/her every time s/he goes to the bathroom. By Sunday night, Mead insists, that toddler will be potty trained!

Renting a baby is *not* advisable!

However, perhaps Susan could have spent two or three weeks with a family with a new baby. (She had no younger brothers and sisters. Her baby sitting experience consisted mainly of evening assignments with sleeping babies.) Most young mothers would welcome help. She could get a taste of real life with an infant. If she could have spent even a weekend taking *full* responsibility for a toddler, she might have had a clearer idea of what it takes to parent a child in the throes of saying "No" to everything, running constantly, and requiring total supervision.

Susan's reaction to her "fostering" experiences might have been positive. Perhaps it would have reinforced her desire to be a mother herself. At the same time, it might have helped her mother realize Susan was, indeed, capable of being a mother even though she was younger than her mother would have liked, and had no husband to assist her.

Or Susan might have found the constant care of either the infant or toddler exhausting. She might have decided that, much as she wanted a child, perhaps that was not the time. She might have decided a father was also needed in her parenting picture.

Vera Casey, director of the Parent-Child Development Center in Berkeley, California, insists she has the best approach to helping high school students realize they aren't ready to be parents. They need to work in an infant center!

She thinks changing diapers, feeding babies, and soothing fussy infants puts a marvelous sense of reality into her students' heads. She agrees, however, that one hour per day of parenting doesn't tell the whole story.

That fact of constant care-giving is an interesting aspect of parenting. Young mothers mention often that everyone -- parents and friends -- promises to help take care of the baby. Before it's born, they can hardly wait to babysit for her. During the first few months the babysitting offers are still frequent.

But when her baby becomes a crawling, into everything youngster some eight months later, the offers to care for her child dwindle to almost nothing. As Erin put it in speaking of eight month old Joanna (Chapter Two), "I guess she's just too old."

ADOPT AN EGG!

Some high school classes take the "Adopt an Egg" approach to teaching students that an infant takes constant care. Each student is given a raw egg. She is encouraged to paint facial features on the egg. Sometimes yarn hair is glued on, and a tiny bassinet made. Each student names her egg.

Then the student is told to treat the egg as if it were a baby. They luck out on the fact that this baby doesn't dirty its diapers, it doesn't get sick, and it doesn't even need to be fed. But it *does* need constant supervision. It must never be left alone. If the "parent" doesn't have her egg-baby with her, she must hire a babysitter.

One girl came to school with a horrified, almost tearful expression. "My baby broke!" she gasped. (She had a double problem -- she lost her "baby," and her purse was a disaster!) Some teachers go so far as to have the student make mock funeral arrangements for a broken egg-baby. Others think this is going a bit far.

But the point is that one's life does change a great deal if one moves almost overnight from being a 16-year-old who loves to shop, party, and goof around to the awesome and total commitment of being a mother. Some young women can do it happily. They seem to be ready for this responsibility. But many pregnant teenagers aren't.

So what's a parent to do?

If your daughter is pregnant and she thinks she
wants to release her baby for adoption, *encourage her to
talk about it.* *Don't* comment, "But how could you give
up your baby?" Suggest to her friends that she is making
her own decision, that it's very hard for her, and you
would appreciate it if they would simply support her, not
try to convince her of anything.

Do you think she is blocking out the realization that
she is, indeed, going to have a real baby? You might start
a discussion of the grief she is almost sure to feel when
she loses her baby. (See Chapter Seven.)

But don't overdo it. She probably is fully aware of
the pain she will experience, is experiencing. She also
probably realizes the pain she would experience in being a
mother *at this time.*

Be aware, too, that you as a grandparent will go
through the grief process. You also need to share your
feelings with someone.

Practical Experience Is Important

If your daughter is pregnant and she thinks she
wants to keep her child, *encourage her to talk about it.*

Also encourage her to spend as much time as possible with other people's babies and toddlers. If there is
an infant center at her school or a daycare center nearby,
strongly urge her to volunteer to help.

Has she "always loved babies"? Has she done a lot
of babysitting? Suggest that during her pregnancy she pre-
tend, each time she cares for someone else's child, that
that little person is really her own. Encourage her to
feel and act as if she were totally responsible for him.

Of course babysitting isn't the same as parenting
one's own child fulltime. As a babysitter, she doesn't
have the responsibility of deciding whether the baby needs
to go to the hospital or whether two aspirin will take care
of her high fever. And if the child is difficult to care for,
she can blame the parents. But if *she* is the parent, obviously she must take these responsibilities fulltime.

But spending as much time as possible with someone else's child while she is pregnant is closer to her future reality than would be living her life as if children didn't exist!

If she hasn't already learned time management skills, help her to do so during pregnancy. Give her a chance to sterilize bottles, make strained baby food, do the laundry.

Help her make lists of the things she'll need to care for baby -- *and* for a toddler. How will she get the money to pay for these things? And just as important, where will she get the space for them? Few families have spare rooms these days. Will the baby be in her room? For how long? Will she keep the confusion of baby things there, or will it spread throughout the house?

If she plans to confine the baby to her room, and expects to live with you for more than a few months, insist that she visit a family with a crawling baby! Babies learn more, develop better if they have as much freedom as is safe. Ideally, an eight month old child will be able to crawl throughout most of his home. Bathrooms should be off limits for safety reasons. But if at all possible, the rest of the house should be baby-proofed.

How will she handle this stage? Or if, as is certainly your right, you don't want your home baby-proofed (you've already been through this stage. . .), what are her plans eight short months after delivery?

Planning sessions don't have to be fights. You are a mother (or father), and your daughter is about to become a mother. Mothers are, by definition (my definition anyhow), adults. As adults, you can discuss these matters!

You do need to be aware of your own limits, and you need to make your daughter aware of those limits. She will cope better if she knows where you are.

"The decision to adopt or keep is based on how a person feels inside. But it is also influenced by the important people in her life," commented nurse-midwife Sen Speroff, Portland, Oregon, whose patients include the young women in a nearby maternity home. "At age 14 or 15, parents are

still very important. If the parents are pushing one way
or another," she emphasized, "it has an effect."

"I have a young patient now," she continued, "who
wants to release her baby for adoption, but her mother is
saying, 'If you release, don't come home because that's
my first grandchild.'"

The parents who truly support their daughter as she
makes her own decision, however, may merit the high
praise bestowed on her mother by Jodie:

> I feel parents are a very important part of
> this. I didn't find out until I was pregnant
> that my mother is the best friend I have. A
> girl really needs her mother -- and her father
> -- at that point. My Mom went through as much
> as I did, maybe more, because I was her daugh-
> ter and this was her grandson.
>
> I think it's because of my mother that I'm
> where I am today. My decision to release my
> baby for adoption was right for me -- but I
> needed my mother's support, and I got it.

If You Work With Pregnant Teenagers

"It's hard for me to think of a very young adolescent being really ready to parent, but I can't say it publicly," commented Jewell Goddard, State Director of the Oregon Boys and Girls Aid Society, at a 1979 conference concerning school age parents. "Many are completely able, others need some support, but we also need to talk about adoption as an option."

Maria Vargas-Pyle, a young social worker in a Los Angeles agency, agrees with him, but cautions, "Adoption is not for everybody. I really have to feel that adoption is for this person. Some girls want you to tell them they should give the child up for adoption. They're just waiting for someone to say, 'Do it, you know you ought to do it.' But we have to help the mother make a decision she can live with. You don't want to talk her into giving up, and then the next thing you know, she has other problems."

Do we ever, as professionals, try too hard to "push" parenthood and relinquishment at the same time? We know it is extremely important that a pregnant teen make her own decision about keeping versus relinquishing.

We know we must not show *our* biases. If we think she is too immature to be a mother, we still must not make that decision for her. And if we think she would cope well with motherhood, our opinion is almost irrelevant if she decides to relinquish her child.

But do we sometimes, in trying for the middle road, end up making it harder for her to make her own decision? In *Becoming an Unwed Mother: A Sociological Account* (1971: Aldine-Atherton), Prudence Rains discusses the dichotomy displayed by the staff at a maternity home.

According to Raines, staff members felt everyone "should" release for adoption, but at the same time they wanted everyone to consider other options. They wanted each young woman to hold and feed her baby. Throughout pregnancy they seemed to encourage their clients to feel like mothers. They then expected them to relinquish for adoption.

True, a decision made in this way can be a strong decision resulting in few regrets later. But is everyone strong enough, and is there any need, to make the decision this difficult? If one of our clients appears to be totally committed to keeping her baby, why should we alienate her by insisting that she consider adoption?

If she "knows" when her pregnancy is verified that adoption is her choice, should she be pushed into parenting classes and Infant Center activities? Real support for her decision might sometimes mean respecting that decision from the beginning. Some young women decide to keep or to relinquish very early in the pregnancy.

Others, however, may not be so sure. Or they may be "sure" because they think either keeping or relinquishing is "the thing to do." Most pregnant teenagers in the United States keep their babies to raise themselves. This has become the cultural norm, and for many young people, going against that norm would be difficult.

In some families, however, relinquishment is the only accepted "solution" to a too-early pregnancy. If a young mother releases her baby for adoption because of pressure from the rest of her family, and not because she thinks this is the right decision, she is apt to face a great deal of emotional trauma after doing so.

Cathy Monserrat, Family Life specialist at the New Futures School in Albuquerque, New Mexico, and co-author of *Teenage Pregnancy, A New Beginning,* advises counselors to look carefully at the motivation seemingly behind the teenage pregnancy. Was it intentional? Does she want a baby badly? If so, relinquishment probably won't work. If she gives this baby up, she may be pregnant again next year. Repeat pregnancy rates are high for teenagers who feel someone else pushed them into either abortion or adoption.

The New Futures School is a large program for pregnant teenagers and school age parents. Students include Black, Anglo, Chicano, and American Indian girls.

"We have been criticized for having a nursery," commented Ms. Monserrat. "People tell us no one will relinquish if they have worked in our nursery, that we're pushing keeping. We find the opposite to be true. I have had students tell me that being around those babies made them decide *not* to keep! Exposure to the nursery actually helped them realize they just weren't ready for parenthood."

Ten to fifteen percent of the New Futures students relinquish each year, according to Ms. Monserrat. Included in the student body are girls from a residential maternity home. Ms. Monserrat thinks this mixture of students creates more open discussion of keeping versus relinquishing.

KEEP OPTIONS OPEN

About 20 percent of the students in the Young Parents Program in the San Juan Unified School District near Sacramento, California, (not a residential program) release their infants for adoption, a higher percentage than occurs in most such programs in California. Jean Colwell, coordinator of the program for five years, gave some possible reasons:

"We do keep options open. Students realize that we actually support girls who are giving up. They know we're not just a nursery. Sometimes girls visit us before enrolling to see if we talk about relinquishment. They don't want to attend a program that is strictly baby-centered. We strongly emphasize on the initial visit that we have girls who keep, girls who relinquish, girls who marry and girls who don't. I insist at the time that everybody be open and supportive of any choice. We don't have cliques of those who release for adoption and those who don't.

"When a student says she is going to relinquish (or keep)," Ms. Colwell added, "we accept that opinion at that time, but we need to realize that throughout pregnancy and shortly thereafter she is apt to vacillate and perhaps change her mind. We must not let ourselves as professionals get locked into her choice either, because at any moment she may change.

"Be aware," she cautioned, "if you don't see her dealing with relinquishment emotionally. If she keeps it at an intellectual level, she hasn't gotten very far into the process of decision making. *And it is a process.* When she starts dealing with it at an emotional level, it's a different thing. And she has got to do this.

"Once I asked a student who was planning to relinquish her baby, 'You really sound like you know what you're doing, but it's all words. I don't hear it coming from feelings.' She assured me she cried a lot at night, but somehow it still seemed to be just words.

"But after she delivered, it hurt her at the feeling level. 'Now I know what you meant,' she told me. The girl who says she is going to relinquish, then changes her mind after delivery generally, in my experience, is a girl who never let herself get to the feeling level in her decision to relinquish."

It's probably healthy for girls who are keeping and girls who are giving up their babies to be together to talk about their options. But because the ones who relinquish are a small minority in many groups, they need extra support. As Jennifer put it in speaking of the "pregnant" class she attended, "The teachers were fine. . .but the kids I could do without. Sometimes I didn't want to go to school because they all thought they were right because they were keeping their babies -- and I was wrong because I was giving mine up. Sometimes I felt really bad about it." Jennifer needed a great deal of extra support from those around her, the kind of support described by Ms. Colwell.

Merle Church, coordinator of the Glendale, California, Teen Mother Program and former president of the

California Alliance Concerned with School Age Parents,
stressed the same thing: "It's like beating a drum over and
over again -- when there is somebody who is relinquishing
or considering it, I continually tell the other girls they are
not to judge her. I do it in as many ways as I can -- like a
broken record -- what's right for Susie isn't necessarily
right for Mary.

"Another thing," continued Ms. Church, "when I'm
with the girl who is planning to relinquish, I try to reinforce positive feelings about herself -- because there is no
way that any decision she makes is going to be painless.
There is just no way -- everything is going to hurt somehow.
Those who do decide to relinquish are usually more mature
in that they can project for five or ten years. They can see
they're not at this time ready emotionally or financially to
raise a child.

"The average school age parent either can't or won't
look into the future," Ms. Church commented. "Neither can
-- or will -- other teenagers. It has to do with intellectual
development; it's part of being an adolescent. That's OK,
except when you put a baby with adolescence, it becomes
much more complicated.

Efforts to help students look into the future and to understand what adoption can mean to the child were described
by Ms. Colwell:

"We frequently bring in people to talk to the class,
people who relinquished recently, others who did so a long
time ago. We've also had an adoptive family share their
lives with the girls -- a father, mother, and their adopted
child. I think these guests help the girls form more positive attitudes about adoption."

Ms. Colwell also suggests the birth mother write a
letter to her baby's adoptive parents or to her child. "This
letter acts as a closure," she explained. "She may not
want to write it when she's eight months pregnant, but two
months after delivery, she may decide to do so."

See Chapter Eight for examples of such letters. Included are letters to the baby, to the adoptive parents, and
a return letter to the birth mother from those parents.

Birth Parents Need Information

"I was glad you did that thing on agency and independent adoption, the pros and cons of it. It made a big impression on me," a student commented. She was referring to a reading assignment on adoption. She had been asked to list the good and bad things about agency vs. independent adoption. At the time she hadn't decided whether to give up her baby or not. (She did relinquish.) Because of her research, she decided to call an agency counselor rather than going directly to a lawyer.

Most teenagers know little or nothing about adoption. Few adults know the agencies available in their area, the pros and cons of agency versus independent adoption.

A flyer containing this information can help a young woman become informed. List the public and private agencies in your area. Describe the services available from each one, and include the name and phone number of a contact person for each. Also describe services available through independent adoption and, again, list a contact person who can give your client more information.

Phyllis, unhappy mother of a two-year-old, has some suggestions for people working with pregnant teenagers:

> You could explain to a person that you do have an option. It wouldn't work to say, "I think you should put your baby up for adoption because you're not ready for it," but you could point out how it will be with a child -- there are too many responsibilities, so many things to take care of, especially when you don't have a father to help. When you're so young, you just don't realize what you're getting into. And you can't depend on welfare to support you all your life. You can't do that because you're not going to get anywhere on welfare.

> I think more people should talk to the girls about adoption. Everybody seems to put people down about adoption, and I think that's why a lot of girls don't do it. A few girls are strong enough, but a lot of them couldn't handle it.

Get someone to come in and tell the girls
about the bad parts of being a parent. Get somebody to talk to them. Tell them it's tough to be
a mother, especially if you're trying to raise a
kid by yourself.

Rap Sessions Can Help

Leading a rap session with pregnant teenagers re-
quires almost superhuman skills in addition to the basic in-
gredient of caring deeply about each girl in the group. A
15-year-old who refused to consider adoption during her
pregnancy, then relinquished her daughter a few months later, spoke disparagingly of the social worker who had led the
rap sessions she attended:

We never told her anything because we thought
she was trying to pry. She asked too many personal questions, and we didn't like her much. She
acted too anxious for us to let her know how we
felt about everything.

If you try to follow Phyllis' advice to "tell the girls
how it is," you may find you have a group of pregnant teenagers who seemingly refuse even to discuss adoption. A
simple starter might be, "Have you thought about adoption?"

Then, if each girl retorts, "Oh, no, that's not for
me," ask how they feel about adoption for other people. This
often starts a discussion.

Utilizing former students as peer counselors is an important aspect of the San Juan Young Parents Program, according to Ms. Colwell. In their rap sessions they try to
include young women who kept their babies and those who
relinquished, those who married and those who remained
single.

"They have gone through the process," explained Ms.
Colwell. "They're part of the group. They look like the
group, and they're catalysts in the process of decision making. They also get a lot out of it themselves because it
gives them much more closure on their own decisions.

"The best peer counselors are those who have thought

about both keeping and relinquishing. If they have gone through the decision making process (neither kept nor relinquished 'because it's the thing to do'), they will be more open to other people's decisions, and that's especially important."

Sometimes teenagers think of adoption agency social workers as "baby stealers." Emphasize the fact that an agency worker is in fact a counselor, that she is there to help a client make the right decision for her, not to talk her into releasing her baby for adoption. Lisa, after talking with an agency worker, commented, "When I've heard about adoption agencies before, I just thought, 'Oh, a baby stealer,' but when you told me about Pat, you called her a counselor. So I wasn't afraid to call her."

The peer counseling described by Ms. Colwell can be an effective part of adoption agency rap sessions too. Explaining to a former client that you think she could help someone else make a decision may elicit positive response. And if you get this kind of program started, current clients will notice, and occasionally someone will see herself in this position in the future. She may volunteer to help or at least be open to an invitation to do so.

RESEARCH ON COUNSELING

A research project carried out in three school districts near Sacramento, California, in 1977-1978 studied the effects of counseling with pregnant adolescents. Their ability to take greater responsibility for the decision-making process, attitudes toward relinquishment, and improvement of positive self-concept after delivery were compared with the amount and kind of counseling received.

Forty students attending the self-contained San Juan program received multiple experiences in counseling. Included were individual counseling, group centered counseling, and group counseling for students considering relinquishment. Peer counselors were used as models in group-centered counseling. The research showed the amount of counseling contact is significantly related to self-concept change. Students in the San Juan treatment group became significantly more positive toward relinquishment while students in the comparison groups (which received only casual or no counseling) exhibited little change. Students with higher over-all self-concept are more likely to have a positive attitude toward relinquishment.

Donna Stringall, psychologist who directed the research, and Ms. Colwell, coordinator of the San Juan program, made the following suggestions based on their research into effective counseling: (1)

"Present the decision making process concerning the pregnancy as a process in which all the alternatives are explored: abortion, marriage, remaining single, relinquishment, or keeping the *child*. (Refer to child rather than baby.) Continually reinforce an open mind toward the process.

"Discourage any negative comments such as 'How can you be so unfeeling as to give away your baby?'

"Explain when a person enters that you want to maintain an atmosphere which allows a free exploration of alternatives so that each person receives support for her decision.

"Don't accept the decision as necessarily a permanent decision. That's where she is today.

"Accept where she is on a given day and expect that change may occur. Don't move faster than where she is. Conversation starters might include statements such as 'Where are you today?' 'What's happening to you now?' 'I notice when you talk about keeping your child, you look down and sound sad.' (The last comment provides feedback on body language.)

"Beware of your biases and how you communicate them verbally and non-verbally.

"Include people in the program as guests or peer counselors who have experienced the various alternatives rather than relying on yourself alone.

---

1. "Counseling and Decision Making in Young Parent Programs." *CACSAP Newsletter*, January, 1978, p. 6.

"Allow the student/client to take responsibility to follow through or initiate an action. Beware of your tendency to become emotionally involved and to take responsibility.

"Approach counseling informally with student who is resistant. Eat lunch with her, take her with you on errands, etc.

"Be the LISTENER, not the talker.

"Remember, we are the models.

"When counseling, choose a private place with no interruptions.

"Include peers with previous experience to model.

"When a parent wishes to talk to the teacher or counselor, include the student if possible.

"Confidentiality is of the utmost importance."

HONESTY IS ESSENTIAL

Being absolutely honest with a birth mother is essential. Maureen, who relinquished her baby independently, was told the adopting parents would keep the name she gave her baby. This didn't happen, and Maureen understood why. But she felt tricked.

Maureen wrote her baby's adoptive parents a letter about a week after his birth. She had been told this would be all right. She described the situation:

I asked if they were going to tell him he was adopted. I said I thought they should, but of course it was up to them. I didn't ask too much. I just said, "Take care of him. Tell him if he ever asks about me that I loved him and that's why I gave him up. I didn't give him up because I didn't want him. I gave him up for his own welfare. A letter came back from the adoptive parents telling me that if I wanted any further contact, I must communicate only through their lawyer.

This upset me -- it was really cold -- because
in the letter I had said this would be the last
time they would hear from me unless they wanted
to. I wish there could have been a little more
trust between us.

What a different feeling Debbie had about her baby's
adoption after she received the letter from his parents! (See
Chapter Eight.)

Support from Hospital Staff

Hospital nurses have a special responsibility with
birth mothers who are relinquishing. Jennifer spoke of the
nurse who talked with her about her own adopted child (Chapter Three). Her friendship during those difficult days meant
a lot to Jennifer.

Ronda, who had already had one baby, reported on the
surprise and disapproval the nurses showed when they
learned she was giving up her second baby. They remembered her from her first delivery, and told her she "should"
keep this one too.

Beth had an especially negative hospital stay:

I stayed in the hospital only two days. That
was *not* a good experience. Because I was relinquishing him, they didn't take me to the maternity ward. That made sense, I guess, but they put
me in a room with three old women who had under-
gone surgery.

First, they couldn't figure out why, if I had
just had a baby, I was in there with them. So I
told them why. They immediately asked how in the
world I could "give up a precious baby." I didn't
need that, and I started crying. I knew I had
made a good decision, but those days immediately
following birth are the hard ones anyhow.

I just didn't need that kind of hassle. I
cried for several hours.

Then my doctor came in. He talked to me and

told me what a great thing I was doing. That
helped a lot.

Before delivery, a young woman planning to relinquish should discuss her choice of rooms with her doctor.
Can she afford a private room if she wants it? If she can't,
or if she doesn't think she'll want to be alone, would she
prefer being with other young mothers, or would it be less
hurtful to be in a different ward?

One usually has very little choice (none, in fact!) in
hospital roommates, but an empathetic nurse can help create
a positive atmosphere for the birth mother who is giving up
her baby. It is usually best for the nurse to explain the situation to the others in the room as tactfully as possible.

One birth mother reported that the minute the hospital staff learned her baby was going to be placed for adoption, he was taken away from the viewing window. No one
could see him, not even his mother, his father, or his grandparents.

"My parents put up such a fuss with the doctor and the hospital administrator," she reported,
"that they finally let us see my baby. But would
you believe when my boy friend, the baby's father,
went in to see him, the nurse picked our baby up,
held him so Joe could see only his bottom, then
instantly the curtain over the viewing window was
dropped! He was really hurt. He stood outside
that window and cried."

When she finally saw her baby, the young mother commented, "Why, he's beautiful now -- and I
thought he was kind of ugly when he was born."

"Is that why you're giving him up, because
he's ugly?" the nurse asked.

And the young mother's entirely unnecessary added
pain was not yet over. When she was ready to go home two
days after delivery, she decided she wanted to see her baby
once more. But she was told he had already gone home with
his adoptive parents. She learned the next day that this was
a lie.

This young mother almost decided to take her baby home with her to "show them." But she realized this would not help her baby, and that the treatment she had endured wasn't his fault.

Another birth mother who delivered in the same hospital, after encountering similar treatment, did decide to take her baby home with her. After one night at home, she called the agency and said, "I have the baby at home, but I'm now ready to relinquish."

As part of an inservice for a large group of obstetrical nurses in the Sacramento area, Ms. Colwell presented a panel of teenagers including single and married mothers and birth mothers who relinquished. The young women shared their personal stories, then expressed some of their frustrations at being treated as kids who don't know what they're doing, called Mrs. when they're not married, and generally treated too often as second-class patients. Response from the nurses was overwhelmingly positive, according to Ms. Colwell.

If you can make time to work with the social worker at your hospital(s), s/he might appreciate lists (frequently updated) of teenage women scheduled to deliver at that hospital. Mark the names of those who are planning to relinquish for adoption. This list plus discussing with the social worker some of the problems the young women have reported may help curtail some of these thoughtlessly hurtful occurrences.

Hospital staff must remember that the birth mother *is* the mother. She has a right to parent while she is there. If she relinquishes, that is her only time to mother this baby, and she must not be told she can't.

Encourage each girl before she delivers to decide how she wants to experience the birth of the baby she may give up. Does she want to give him a name? He needs a name for his original birth certificate as well as the name his adoptive parents will give him. His birth parents can give him that name. Does she want to see her baby? Will she hold him? Feed him? Who will be permitted to see her baby?

"We find it helps to suggest she fantasize leaving the baby," commented Ms. Colwell. "We ask her to picture this leaving. If they make these decisions before delivery, they are so much better prepared for the actual relinquishment."

GUILT FEELINGS IN ADOPTION

Sen Speroff, certified nurse-midwife in Portland, Oregon, discussed a patient who had not had "closure" when she gave up her baby. When Ms. Speroff first saw her, Jane was ambivalent about releasing. She said she felt guilty thinking about adoption because she should not have had her baby at this time. Therefore she should keep it.

But she did relinquish her child. When she came back for her postpartum checkup, she was a month late. She said she hadn't wanted to come in because the hospital reminded her of her baby. Then she burst into tears. Ms. Speroff continues:

"I asked her about the birth. Did the baby look like you? What do you see as the personality of your baby? How did you adopt? (Independently through a lawyer.) What do you know about the family? (Nothing.) Do you feel good about that? (No.)

"Not knowing anything made her wonder if it was OK. She had absolutely no information, just that it was a 'good' set of parents who wanted a child. She didn't name the child because she didn't know she could name him. She didn't write a letter.

"I think guilt may have been an important part of this situation. We talked about her negative feelings and the hurting. I like to do a reversal of that. I say, 'I see two things in a person like you -- first, that adoption was not easy, it wasn't an act of abandonment. It was an act of love, a sacrifice you made. Second, what do people around you think of this?' She said they think of it as abandonment.

"But at this point I could see a glimmer in her eyes that yes, she did give him up because she loved him. I really push the idea that she is a good mother now, and she will be a good mother later. Hopefully her self image will be boosted because of that.

"The woman I worry about," Ms. Speroff continued, "is the one who releases and says life can go on, it was no big thing. I stress most the options, the rights, and that the woman must be aware of the negative aspects of adoption. She must turn that hurt around into something positive.

"We take pictures of the baby, often do full shots of delivery. Birth mothers want these, they want the name tag, the footprints. These memories can help."

Do Only Anglos Adopt?

Conventional wisdom in some areas is that Black and Mexican American birth parents never consider adoption. Yet California statistics show the proportion of white children placed for adoption decreased from 70.4 percent in 1970 to 55.3 percent in 1975 (State of California, 1978: "Characteristics of Relinquishment Adoptions in California 1970-1975). The percentage of children of Mexican American or Black ethnic origin more than doubled, increasing from 8.1 percent to 18.8 percent total for the two groups. Percentage of children with mixed ethnic origin released for adoption stayed about the same: 16 percent in 1970, 18.3 percent in 1975.

The situation is changing. Adoption agency workers in Los Angeles County report a significant number of Black and Chicano babies being released for adoption.

Ms. Monserrat stated that New Futures birth mothers in Albuquerque who relinquish include Black, Chicano, Native American, and Anglo students. An increasing number of Black clients at the Florence Crittenton Services in Charlotte, North Carolina, are releasing, according to Lou Watson, administrative assistant.

Total placements (527) through the County of Los Angeles Department of Adoptions for the fiscal year 1978-1979 were 46 percent Anglo, 26 percent Black, 23 percent Mexican American, and 4 percent other ethnic groups, according to Laine Waggoner, Public Relations Coordinator, Department

of Adoptions, County of Los Angeles. About the same percentage in each ethnic group occurred when only children
under age two at time of relinquishment were considered.

No matter which ethnic group(s) you work with, you
want to know something about and, above all, to respect
each individual's cultural background. However, it is *not*
wise to prejudge a person on the basis of the ethnic group to
which she appears to belong, i.e., to assume that because
she is Black, she "of course" will keep her baby.

Teachers sometimes say, in speaking of their students in schools in predominantly Black areas, "None of my
students would ever consider adoption. It's not part of
their culture." This may be true of many of their clients,
perhaps most of them. You may work with 100 pregnant
teenagers who "know" they're keeping the baby. But if you
have one student/client who, after deciding against abortion,
isn't positive she's ready to be a mother, that client needs
your help in realizing she does have another option. She
isn't trapped into too-early motherhood because she's pregnant. She, too, has the option of adoption.

And you can reassure her that there are Black,
Chicano, and other minority couples waiting to adopt, couples who would give her baby the love and care she wants
for him. You can also assure her that most infants, according to California statistics, are placed with adopting parents
with the same ethnic background as the child. If she requests such a placement for her child, her request will probably be granted.

The birth parent today may help choose her baby's
adoptive parents, not only if she "goes independent," but also if she relinquishes through a private or public agency. A
Los Angeles County Department of Adoptions brochure
states, "We let birth parents play an important part in the
selection of an adoptive family for their child from the agency's many approved families." The statement is printed in
bold type and underlined for emphasis.

In addition, a cautious statement is added: "Consideration can be given to those birth parents who would like to
meet the prospective adoptive family before placement."

OPEN RECORD CONTROVERSY

Today much controversey surrounds the question of adult adoptees searching for their birth parents and birth parents looking for the children they have relinquished. But why are we so afraid of open records? If a birth mother was promised anonymity twenty years ago, it could be disturbing to have a grown son walk in unannounced one day. But most people advocating open records appear to want some kind of national registry to help in such a search coupled with an intermediary plan. In such a plan, a third party would contact either the birth parent or the adoptee to learn if a reunion is desired or would be acceptable.

Most research (as reported in *The Adoption Triangle* by Sorosky, Baran, and Pannor, and "Report of Research Project -- The Changing Face of Adoption," Children's Home Society of California) shows the majority of birth parents, adoptees, and adoptive parents comfortable with the idea of a reunion between birth parents and adoptees.

Yet a recent study of attitudes of *adoption agencies* toward open records was quite negative. "The Sealed Adoption Record Controversy," published in 1976 by the Child Welfare League of America, Inc., reports the results of a survey in which questionnaires were returned by 163 adoption agencies in the United States and Canada. Data is presented concerning adoptees and birth parents who returned to these agencies requesting information about their birth parents/relinquished children.

Although most agencies felt that such a search was a natural hunt for personal identity, they didn't believe that laws should be changed to allow adult adoptees access to the information -- in court or agency records, now or in the future. The major reason given was to protect the anonymity of the birth parents.

This appears to be an example of agencies thinking *for* birth parents rather than letting birth parents make their own decisions regarding reunions with their relinquished children.

Charlotte De Armond, Public Affairs Director for Children's Home Society of California, produced the film,

"Growing Up Together," in 1974. It presents case studies of four young single mothers and their children. Before making the film, Ms. De Armond interviewed 152 girls who were keeping their babies.

She asked each one, "Did you ever consider adoption?" Over and over she heard the same answer, "I might have, but I couldn't face never seeing or knowing anything about my child again."

"If we could change our laws to provide for an exchange of identification when adoptees become adults and when they and their birth parents desire it, I think we could place a lot more children for adoption," she commented.

IMPORTANCE OF YOUR FEELINGS

As professionals, we must consider the feelings we have about adoption. Do some of us consider it abandonment? Or do we think it's "so sad" to see a 15-year-old keep her baby? What are our biases?

Have you ever had an unwanted pregnancy? Perhaps you need to consider your feelings toward that pregnancy and how these feelings may affect the way you look at the whole issue.

If you have ever adopted -- or attempted to adopt -- a child or have had a close friend who did so, this experience may have created strong pro-adoption feelings. If your client is a young birth mother, the adoptive parents waiting out there are *not* your primary concern!

Your primary concern is your client -- that young birth parent facing the most difficult decision she may ever have to make. Should she become a mother to the baby with whom she is bonding throughout pregnancy -- and face the highly probable result of too little education, never enough money, a life irretrievably changed because of her early entry into parenthood?

Or should she relinquish her baby for adoption and face the grief she will feel at losing her child, grief that may linger for a long time?

A hard decision for anyone to make -- and to a 14-, 15-, or 16-year-old, it can seem insurmountable. If you work with one or many pregnant adolescents, your responsibility to help *her* make *her own* decision is a mind boggling challenge.

Whatever your role -- as teacher, nurse, counselor, social worker, doctor, independent adoption facilitator, perhaps adoptive parent or the parent of a birth parent -- please remember you are dealing with a mother who cares deeply about her baby, who undoubtedly wants the best life possible for her child.

Many teenagers feel they can provide that "best possible life" for their children -- but others need to be assured they indeed have the option of adoption.

BIBLIOGRAPHY

The following books were selected because of their interest to or information about pregnant adolescents. Several recently published books on adoption are listed, books which give good background information on adoption generally. However, few books designed for adopted children or for adoptive parents are included.

Most of these books contain some information about decision making and/or adoption as it relates to birth parents. In most cases, however, references to birth parents who might release for adoption are a relatively small part of the resource.

Ashdown-Sharp, Patricia. *A Guide to Pregnancy and Parenthood for Women on Their Own.* 1977. Vintage Books. New York: Random House.

Much newer than Pierce's *Single and Pregnant,* this book includes an excellent, up-to-date treatment of abortion as well as a chapter on adoption. Generally, however, it seems to be directed more to older readers than to teenagers, but it is a good additional resource. A study guide for the book is included in *Parenting Preschoolers* by Lindsay.

Baker, Nancy C. *Baby Selling: The Scandal of Black Market Adoptions.* 1978. New York: The Vanguard Press.

This very readable book, as its title implies, is an expose of black market adoptions in the United States. The situation is discussed from the standpoints of the adoptive parents, the birth parents, and the "baby brokers." Outlawing independent adoptions is not the solution, according to Baker. There is a real need for independent adoption to continue, she points out. Instead, strong federal legislation as well as improved state laws are needed to prohibit

the crime of black market adoption. The final chapter discusses alternatives to the black market for people wishing to
adopt a child. The book's Appendix includes a 26-page list-
ing of adoption sources.

Barr, Linda, and Catherine Monserrat. *Teenage Pregnancy: A New Beginning.* 1978. New Futures, Inc., 2120 Louisiana NE, Albuquerque, NM 87110.

A book written specifically for pregnant adolescents, *Teenage Pregnancy: A New Beginning* is an 80-page illustrated
textbook. Topics include prenatal health care, nutrition
during pregnancy, fetal development, preparation for labor
and delivery, decision-making, emotional effects of adolescent pregnancy, and others. The authors have obviously
known, worked with, and loved many school age parents. The
book is written for them (and often quotes them), not for the
assumed-to-be-nonpregnant general high school population at
which most textbooks are directed. It is written at a sixth
grade reading level.

_____. *Working with Childbearing Adolescents: A Guide
for Use with Teenage Pregnancy, A New Beginning.* 1980. New
Futures, Inc.

This book is designed specifically for professionals who
work with pregnant adolescents. The introductory chapter
presents an overview of teen pregnancy and parenthood in the
United States. In addition, adolescent development and sexuality are explored. The book also contains a complete
course outline with lesson plans and resource material to
accompany each chapter in the student text. Learning strat-
egies are applicable to both classroom and individualized
study. The authors have included their experiences, ideas,
and insights gained through working with pregnant adolescents.

Benet, Mary Kathleen. *The Politics of Adoption.* 1976. New York:
The Free Press. A Division of Macmillan Publishing Company, In-
corporated.

The history of adoption through the ages and around the
world is described and compared with adoption practices today. Inter-country and inter-racial adoption are discussed
as are the adopters, the birth parents, and the adoptees.
The author attempts to "trace the influence of attitudes on
practice and of practice on law" (p. 13). "The Baby Famine"
is discussed in the first chapter.

Bloomfield, Harold. *How to Survive the Loss of a Love.* 1977: A
Bantam Book. Boston: Houghton Mifflin Company.

This short paperback contains poetry and other easy reading
selections on grief and the process of loss. The book

explains each grief process in an easily understood and beautiful manner. The book could be a valuable addition to a study unit on adoption.

Burgess, Linda Cannon. *The Art of Adoption.* 1976. Washington, D.C.: Acropolis Books.

Ms. Burgess, who was responsible for more than 900 adoptions in Washington, D.C., based her book on interviews in 45 homes where 146 children she had placed were growing up. She discusses adoption from the viewpoint of the adopting parents, birth mothers, biological fathers, involved grandparents, foster mothers, and, of course, the adopted children. Each chapter is illustrated with human interest stories drawn from her wide experience as executive director of an adoption agency. She also includes a discussion of adult adoptees searching for their birth parents.

Children's Home Society of California. *The Changing Face of Adoption: Report of Research Project.* 1977. CHS of California, 3100 West Adams Boulevard, Los Angeles, CA 90018.

In 1976, CHS published and distributed *The Changing Face of Adoption.* The magazine was devoted to the many issues surrounding the question of what rights, if any, adult adoptees have to information that was "sealed" by law when their adoption was approved by the court. Included were questionnaires to be returned by birth parents, adoptees, and adoptive parents. Almost 1900 questionnaires were returned and tabulated. This 36-page booklet reports the results of this research.

Eleven Million Teenagers -- What Can Be Done About the Epidemic of Adolescent Pregnancies in the U.S. 1976. Publication of the Alan Guttmacher Institute, The Research and Development Division of Planned Parenthood Federation of America, 515 Madison Avenue, New York, NY 10022. Price: $2.50.

Basic facts about adolescent sexuality, pregnancy, and childbearing are well described and illustrated through many colorful charts in the first section of this 64 page booklet. Comparisons are made in the second section, again with the use of many charts, of the results of having a baby while a young teenager rather than waiting five years. The third section titled "What Is Being Done" describes the lack of adequate sex education in the schools, the high number of teens who get inadequate or no prenatal care, the lack of daycare for their babies, the lack of birth control services for many teens, and the rising teenage abortion rate coupled with the fact that "at least 125,000 teenagers still lack access to abortion services." What could be done is then described. A number of concrete workable suggestions are listed, followed by an "Afterword" by Daniel Callahan in which he discusses the reality of teenage sexuality.

Furstenberg, Frank F., Jr. *Unplanned Parenthood: The Consequences of Teenage Childbearing.* 1976. The Free Press, Macmillan Publishing Company.

A six-year study of 400 adolescent mothers was done in Baltimore 1966-1972. It presents solid statistics to back up the following conclusion: "The adolescent mothers consistently experienced great difficulty in realizing their life plans, when compared with their classmates who did not become pregnant premaritally in their early teens. Marital instability, school disruption, economic problems, and difficulty in family size regulation and childrearing were some of the complications brought on by their premature, unscheduled childbearing." The study focused not only on the 400 young mothers, but also on their partners, children, and parents. The study also compared the experiences of the young mothers with those of a peer group who managed to avoid premature parenthood.

Howard, Marion. *Only Human - Teenage Pregnancy and Parenthood.* 1976. New York: The Seabury Press, Inc. 1979. Paper, Avon Books.

An easily read story about three young couples expecting their first child. Interspersed throughout the story is a running commentary about the developmental aspects of both young women and young men as they go through the pregnancy and parenting experience. Professionals reading the book are apt to gain some new insights into the feelings and concerns of young parents, and may, after reading it, find themselves more sensitive to their clients.

Koschnick, Kay (ed.). *Having a Baby.* 1975. New Readers Press, Laubach Literacy, Inc., P.O. Box 131, Syracuse, NY 13210.

Having a Baby is an excellent resource for high school students learning about pregnancy and parenting through the first few weeks after delivery. It is written on a fifth grade reading level, but it is designed for adult readers. Chapters of the book are also available as separate booklets. One booklet, "Pregnant and Unmarried" by Maxine Phillips, discusses adoption as an alternative. The book and pamphlets present reliable information in an interesting manner.

Lee, Joanna. *I Want to Keep My Baby.* 1977. New York: A Signet Book, New American Library.

Some young birth mothers may recognize parts of themselves in Sue Ann as she realizes she is pregnant, then fantasizes about marriage to the baby's father. Instead, her boy friend takes off, leaving her to face pregnancy and motherhood alone. When she mentions the idea of adoption, both her mother and her minister are horrified. So she keeps her

baby. . .for six months. The book is a well written novel
about the realities of becoming a mother at 15, and the difficult option of relinquishing for adoption at that time.

Lindsay, Jeanne Warren. *Parenting Preschoolers: Curriculum Help
    and Study Guides (Teacher's Guide); Parenting Preschoolers:
    Study Guides for Child Care Books (Student Manual).* 1978.
    Morning Glory Press, 6595 San Haroldo Way, Buena Park, CA 90620.

For use *with* other already-published books, *Parenting Preschoolers* contains study guides for ten books dealing with
parenting small children. The study guides are easy to use
and understand, and may be used for individualized study as
well as guides to group discussions. Included is a study
guide for *A Guide to Pregnancy and Parenthood for Women on
Their Own* by Ashdown-Sharp, a book which contains a chapter
on the adoption alternative.

_____. *They'll Read If It Matters: Study Guides for
Books About Pregnancy and Parenting; You'll Read If It Matters, A Student Manual.* 1977. Morning Glory Press.

Format of this set of books is similar to *Parenting Preschoolers*. Study guides are included for fifteen of the
best, already-in-print books about pregnancy and parenting
an infant. Books covered include *Having a Baby* by Koschnick
(ed) and *Single and Pregnant* by Pierce, each of which contains a section on adoption. *They'll Read If It Matters* also
contains an annotated bibliography of sixty other books about
sex education, birth control, pregnancy and birth, prenatal
nutrition, babies and parents, and personal experience.

March of Dimes Birth Defects Foundation. *Preparenthood Education
    Program.* 1978. Supply Division, MOD, 1275 Mamaroneck Avenue,
    White Plains, NY 10605.

PEP — the March of Dimes Preparenthood Education Program --
is one of the best resources dealing with teenage pregnancy.
The materials are designed to help teenage girls (and boys)
learn good nutrition and health care for themselves and
their unborn babies and to explore some of the emotional and
physical aspects of pregnancy. Decision-making is discussed.

McNamara, Joan. *The Adoption Adviser.* 1975. New York: Hawthorn
    Books, Inc. An Information House book.

The book is designed for adoptive parents and has little to
offer the birth mother. It does, however, contain the name
and address of the agency in each state which has listings
of licensed adoption agencies within the state. It also
charts state adoption laws including which states permit independent adoptions and which states do not. Laws in some
states may have changed since the book was published.

Meezan, William, Sanford Katz, and Eva Manoff Russo. *Adoptions Without Agencies: A Study of Independent Adoptions*. 1978. New York: Child Welfare League of America, Inc.

Independent adoption as experienced by the birth parents and the adoptive parents was thoroughly researched. The book is the report of that research. The legal and psychological risks of independent adoption are outlined, but the authors do not recommend outlawing all independent adoption. Rather, they suggest a number of changes in agency and independent adoption practices, changes which could make adoption more satisfying to all those involved. The book includes a complete review and an analysis of the laws of all the states as they relate to independent adoption. It is an excellent resource for adoption information.

Peck, Richard. *Don't Look and It Won't Hurt*. 1973. New York: Avon Books.

A young girl named Carol describes her feelings as her sister leaves to continue her pregnancy out of town. Her sister's decision to relinquish her baby for adoption affects Carol deeply.

Pierce, Ruth I. *Single and Pregnant*. 1971. Boston: The Beacon Press.

Although not a new book, this is still an excellent resource for students who are pregnant, who know someone who is, or who worry they might be. Each of the alternatives available to a single, pregnant woman -- adoption, abortion, marriage, single parenthood -- is discussed in detail. A study guide for *Single and Pregnant* is included in *They'll Read If It Matters* by Lindsay.

Sorosky, Arthur D., M.D., Annette Baran, and Reuben Pannor. *The Adoption Triangle: The Effects of the Sealed Record on Adoptees, Birth Parents, and Adoptive Parents*. 1978. Garden City, NY: Anchor Press/Doubleday.

The authors re-evaluate adoption policies. Interviews and correspondence with hundreds of adoptees, birth parents, and adoptive parents are utilized to get at the central problems and issues -- the fears and concerns of both adoptive and birth parents and the psychological needs of adult adoptees. The authors see adoption as a life-long process, and they suggest that we need to reform our attitudes and policies regarding adoption. They discuss the effects of reunion experiences between adoptees and their birth parents.

Tanner, Ira J. *The Gift of Grief: Healing the Pain of Everyday Losses*. 1976. New York: Hawthorn Books, Inc.

Tanner is not writing specifically about adoption, but the

Loss of a child through relinquishment is indeed cause for grief. The grieving and healing cycle he describes applies as well to a birth parent's grief for the loss of her/his child as it does to other major losses. A young parent might find the book a great help as s/he deals with his/her grief.

Thompson, Jean. *The House of Tomorrow.* 1974. New York: Harper and Row Pub., Inc.

The author writes movingly about her struggle over what to do about her pregnancy and future baby. Her experiences in a maternity home are described, experiences quite different from those of most school age pregnant women today. The story actually took place in the 1960s in California. Her decision was to release her baby for adoption.

Walsworth, Nancy, and Patricia Bradley. *Coping with School Age Motherhood.* 1979. New York: Richards Rosen Press, Inc.

Written as a first person account of a year in a school age mothers program, the book consists of twelve non-fiction case studies of pregnant teenagers, school age mothers, fathers (two examples), and, in one chapter, a teenage mother's own mother. In each vignette, the program's teacher describes the young parent's arrival in the S.A.M. program, her experiences and growth while there, and in some cases, the birth of the baby. Three accounts deal with young women who relinquish their babies for adoption. Decision making processes dealing with keeping vs. relinquishing are touched upon in several other stories.